The Story of Norton Barracks
Home of the Worcestershire Regiment

The Story of Norton Barracks
Home of the Worcestershire Regiment

by
Stan Jobson, MA

Logaston Press

LOGASTON PRESS
Little Logaston Woonton Almeley
Herefordshire HR3 6QH
logastonpress.co.uk

First published by Logaston Press 2015
Copyright Text © Stan Jobson 2015
Copyright Photographs © the Mercian Regiment Museum (Worcestershire) 2015
Registered Charity No.276510

ISBN 978 1 906663 92 6

Typeset by Logaston Press
and printed and bound in Glasgow
by Bell & Bain Ltd

CONTENTS

Acknowledgements

This book could not have come about if the men and women who were part of the history of Norton Barracks had not shared their knowledge and recorded their experiences; to them must go any credit for the greater part of this work. My contribution has been to link this material and to include the background against which these personal stories are set.

The main sources have been the regimental histories, the records, the files and other documents that are held in the museum archives. The most interesting of these are the personal accounts of those who have served or worked at Norton. Photographs are taken primarily from the collection contained within the archives or from other regimental publications, unless otherwise acknowledged.

Because recent history is more readily available, the personal profiles included in this book are mostly those of men who have served the Regiment in more recent times and who survive in regimental folklore, in history, or in living memory. Many old soldiers will have their own idea of who else should have been included in such profiles, and I can only offer sincere apologies to the many officers and men who could have been recognised in this way but who have had to be omitted due to lack of accessible information.

My thanks go to *The Worcester Standard*, *The Worcester Evening News*, and *The Black Country Bugle* and to the magazine *Worcestershire Now*, for permission to use written extracts or photographs. I am grateful to Louis Scully for the use of his Worcestershire Regiment website (www.worcestershireregiment.com), to Michael Hargreave Mawson for permission to use the portrait of Colonel F.F. Hunter from his personal collection, and to the University of Birmingham for permission to use extracts and a photograph from Raymond Priestley's papers.

I am particularly indebted to Mrs Edith Price and Mr Alec Mackie for reading and commenting on the draft document and to John Lowles for sharing his knowledge, and for his invaluable help and support during the production of this book. Finally, thanks to Andy and Karen Johnson at Logaston Press for their expertise, help and guidance in bringing this book to completion.

I have endeavoured to ensure that no copyright infringements have occurred, and apologise for any omissions, transgressions or errors that I have unwittingly made.

Stan Jobson
Worcester, May 2015

PREFACE

During most of his career a soldier leads a nomadic existence as he travels the world, but an infantryman used to start and finish his service in the same place, his regimental depot, and frequently returned there over the years to meet his former comrades at reunions.

Norton Barracks, as the depot of the Worcestershire Regiment, therefore has a special place in the memory of many who served there. Regular recruits and conscripts alike recalled their apprehension at arriving for the first time at the forbidding-looking Keep, and the shock, for many, of leaving home for the first time to enter a disciplined institutional environment. This was replaced by the feeling, by the time they completed their training at the barracks, of accomplishment and comradeship engendered among their group on achieving a shared goal. For many of the younger instructors a tour of duty at the depot provided a welcome break from the hurly-burly of battalion life away from home, and an opportunity for a more settled existence. Many married local girls. For the older soldiers nearing the end of their service, a position at the depot provided the opportunity to put down roots before their transfer to civilian life.

Training staff were responsible for carrying out the induction and basic training of recruits for many infantry regiments, as well as conducting specialist training for other arms of the service. Regimental headquarters staff performed the role of guardians of regimental records, keepers of regimental property and administrators of all regimental matters. The depot was for many years the home of the Regimental Archives and Museum, and staff acted as both archivists and curators in addition to their regimental duties.

The story of Norton Barracks, of the men and women who served there and the events that took place throughout its existence, are an integral and important part of the history of the Worcestershire Regiment, so some reference to regimental history in the wider sense is inevitable.

Stan Jobson has done a skilful job in pulling together the memories of those soldiers and civilians who worked, played or lived at the barracks, and the Mercian Regiment Museum (Worcestershire) trustees are grateful to him for providing this record of life at Norton.

John Lowles
Worcester, May 2015

This book has been commissioned by the
Mercian Regiment Museum (Worcestershire)
following an anonymous bequest for this purpose

THE WORCESTERSHIRE REGIMENT
DOWN THE YEARS

The formation of the Worcestershire Regiment in 1881 brought together three disparate elements which had hitherto existed as separate entities. They were:

> The regular regiments formed as Farrington's and Charlemont's Regiments of Foot in January 1694 and 1702, which in 1751 were re-designated as the 29th and 36th Regiments. In 1784 they were assigned for recruiting purposes to Worcestershire and Herefordshire respectively.
>
> The Worcestershire Militia, a citizen force which had existed sporadically in various guises since Saxon times but which was established on a permanent basis in 1770. Militia men were billeted, normally in Worcester, once a year each summer for 28 days training and were liable to be called out in the event of riot, insurrection or the threat of invasion. By 1881 the Militia consisted of two battalions, and had a small administrative centre in St George's Square in Worcester.
>
> The Administrative battalions of the Worcestershire Volunteer Corps which had been formed from 1859 in the principal towns in the county and met, usually weekly, in the Volunteer drill halls in their home towns.

Neither the 29th and 36th Regiments nor their successor battalions ever served together in the same military formation. The purpose of combining them was to enable one to serve at home and supply reinforcements to the other serving abroad. The purpose of combining them with the Militia was to facilitate regular recruiting from the Militia.

The first occupants of the barracks in 1878 were the depot companies of the 29th and 36th regiments, which had until then been co-located with their parent regiments when the latter were based at home, and had remained at home on recruiting duties when their regiments were abroad. They were followed shortly afterwards by the Militia permanent staff.

In 1970 the Worcestershire Regiment was amalgamated with the Sherwood Foresters and Norton became the Regimental HQ of the new regiment, the Worcestershire and Sherwood Foresters Regiment. In 2007 a further amalgamation took place when the regiment joined with the Cheshire and Staffordshire Regiments to form the Mercian Regiment.

After over 130 years, the military presence on the Norton site came to an end early in 2011 when the Regimental HQ was closed and its function was moved to the Regimental HQ of the Mercian Regiment at Lichfield. All that remains of the military footprint is the imposing Keep block – now converted into flats, the old Sergeants' Mess – now a sports club, a row of houses along Regiment Close which had been built as married quarters and the street names on the housing estate on the former barrack and camp site, the streets having been named after some of the regiment's battle honours.

The terms battalion, regiment, brigade and division when applied to the infantry can be confusing to the layman. The makeup of such formations changed over time as the Army's structure changed. Until 1881 the term 'regiment' denoted a formation of a number of service companies and depot companies; after 1881 it denoted a grouping of one or more battalions. An infantry brigade in the First World War consisted of four infantry battalions numbering about 5,000 men under the command of a Brigadier. An infantry division was a fighting formation normally comprising three fighting brigades as well as artillery, engineers and ancillary troops, a total of about 20,000 men.

In the mid Victorian period British infantry regiments had usually consisted of a single regular battalion. When not at war the battalion would serve overseas, often for several years, policing the empire, looking after trade routes and British interests throughout the world, or would remain at home on recruitment and training duties, garrisoning home establishments and available to respond to any operation, public duty or emergency that might require a military presence. Although the formation of regiments varied, the majority of line infantry battalions of the day comprised six field or 'fighting' companies and one or more depot companies. Following the Army reforms of the late 19th century the formation of regiments again changed.

During the First World War a battalion, commanded by a Lieutenant-Colonel, numbered over 1,000 men, including about 30 officers when fully established. As well as Battalion Headquarters it contained four field companies designated A to D.[1] Each company, commanded by a Major or senior Captain, numbered 227 men. The company was divided into four platoons each under a junior officer, a Lieutenant or Second-Lieutenant commanding about 54 men. Each platoon was made up of four sections of 12 men under the command of a non-commissioned officer. Platoons were the basic fighting unit of the regiment and their composition was changed to meet the changing demands of warfare. In 1914, for example, the infantry platoon was made up of four rifle sections but by 1917 it consisted of an integrated fire team of rifle, Lewis gun, and grenade and rifle grenade sections. By 1918 it had lost its rifle section and became a firepower platoon comprising two grenade and two Lewis gun sections, an innovation which proved very effective during infantry attacks in the final months of the war.[2]

A summary of the evolution of the Worcestershire Regiment

(Worcs Regt = Worcestershire Regiment; Bn = Battalion)

1694	Farrington's Regiment →								
1702	Charlemont's Regiment →								
1751	29th Regiment →	36th Regiment →							
1770					Worcestershire Militia →				
1784	29th (Worcestershire) Regiment →	36th (Herefordshire) Regiment →							
1798							Worcestershire Volunteer Companies	Worcestershire Volunteer companies	
1859							1st Admin Bn Worcestershire Volunteer Corps →	2nd Admin Bn Worcestershire Volunteer Corps	
1874					1st Militia Bn	2nd Militia Bn	→		
1881	1st Bn Worcs Regt →	2nd Bn Worcs Regt →			3rd (Militia) Bn Worcs Regt	4th (Militia) Bn Worcs Regt	1st (Volunteer) Bn Worcs Regt →	2nd (Volunteer) Bn Worcs Regt →	
1900			3rd Bn Worcs Regt →	4th Bn Worcs Regt →	5th (Militia) Bn Worcs Regt	6th (Militia) Bn Worcs Regt	→	→	
1908					5th (Special Reserve) Bn Worcs Regt →	6th (Special Reserve) Bn Worcs Regt →	7th Bn Worcs Regt Territorial Force →	8th Bn Worcs Regt Territorial Force →	
1914-19					→	→			14 New Army Battalions
1922			Disbanded		Disbanded	Disbanded			
1939-45				Disbanded					4 Wartime Battalions
1947		Disbanded						Disbanded	
1967							Disbanded		
1970	1st Bn Worcestershire & Sherwood Foresters Regt →								
2007	2nd Bn Mercian Regt								

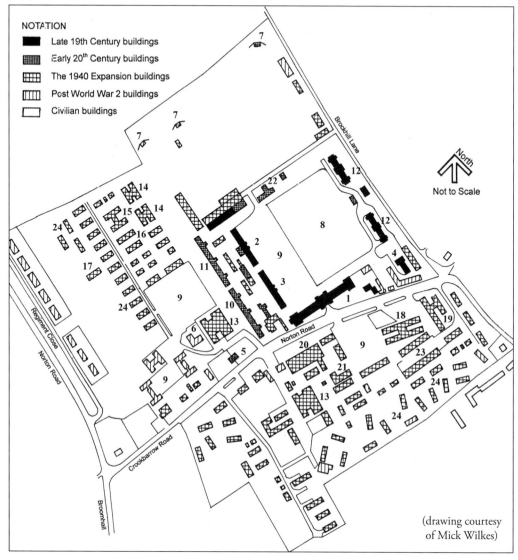

NOTATION
- ■ Late 19th Century buildings
- ▦ Early 20th Century buildings
- ▦ The 1940 Expansion buildings
- ▥ Post World War 2 buildings
- ▢ Civilian buildings

North
Not to Scale

(drawing courtesy
of Mick Wilkes)

The Development of Norton Barracks
Key to numbers on the plan

1 The Keep
2 Charlemont Block
3 Farrington Block
4 Hospital
5 Regimental Cottages
6 RC Chapel & C of E
   Church Hut
7 Butts
8 Cricket Ground

9 Parade Grounds
10 Higginson Block
11 Jacob Block
12 Other Ranks Married Qtrs
13 Cookhouses
14 WOs & Sergeants Living
    Qtrs
15 WOs & Sergeants' Mess
16 Drill Sheds

17 Bath House
18 Single Officers' Qtrs
19 Officers' Mess
20 Junior Ranks Club
21 NAAFI
22 Sergeants' Mess
23 Motor Transport Garage
24 Living Huts

1 BUILDING AND OCCUPATION, 1874-98

'Amid much change Norton Barracks represents all that is permanent in the life of the Regiment.'   Lt-Col the Lord Birdwood.[1]

The construction of Norton Barracks, which began in 1874, was part of a country-wide programme for the provision of permanent barracks for infantry regiments. Its completion in 1878 and the formation of the Worcestershire Regiment in the early 1880s were the culmination of a series of reforms started by Lord Cardwell, Secretary of State for War between 1868 and 1874, which were designed to improve the Army's efficiency.

The reforms resulted in a costly building programme which saw 21 new barracks or depots being built by 1880, including that at Norton Juxta Kempsey. Each provided accommodation for single officers and soldiers, married quarters, a school, a hospital and stabling for horses, in addition to the necessary training facilities.

As well as introducing linked battalions (after 1881 a regiment would usually comprise two or more battalions), the reforms included an initiative founded on the German idea of drafting volunteers and conscripts into regiments based on a defined locality or region. This was seen as a means of encouraging recruitment by introducing closer integration of county militia and regular units, at the same time as providing improved training facilities resulting from the new barracks. Cardwell proposed that Britain and Ireland would be divided into 66 infantry districts, 12 artillery districts and 2 cavalry districts. Each district would have a Regimental Depot where recruits would undergo basic training.[2]

A circular dated 21 April 1873 contained a warrant, (dated 8 April 1873), stating that Queen Victoria had sanctioned the formation of District Brigades. The Worcestershire Militia, to which a 2nd Battalion was to be added, was brigaded with the 29th (Worcestershire) Regiment, the 36th (Herefordshire) Regiment and the Herefordshire Militia; the whole forming the 22nd Brigade under Colonel Robert White, CB. New barracks were to be built for the accommodation of the Brigade Depot at Norton Juxta Kempsey, about three miles from Worcester.[3]

Land Purchase and Construction, 1872-77

Following the decision to build the new barracks the War Department had, in 1872, purchased a 20.5-acre site at Norton for £3,500. The design incorporated the recommendations of a Royal Commission of 1861. This reported on the sanitary conditions of soldiers living in military barracks, and found that the mortality rate of soldiers between 20 and 40 years of age was 17.11 per thousand. Compared to a civilian male death rate of only 9.8 per thousand, this was seen as a terrible reflection on soldiers' living conditions. The commission's report contained a number of recommendations to ensure an improvement in living standards, including the provision of a minimum of 17 cubic metres of air space, and 5.6 square metres of floor space per man, as well as improved toilet facilities, bath houses and purpose-built gymnasia. The commission's recommendations were accepted by Parliament, but progress on their implementation was nevertheless both slow and unreliable;[4] the building programme was, as a consequence, prolonged in its development. Partly as a result of the building programme, the improvement in sanitary conditions was such that by 1897 the mortality rate of soldiers in barracks had dropped to 3.42 men per thousand,[5] a considerable improvement over the 1861 figure, but one that had taken over 30 years to achieve.

Work on building the barracks was started by the contractor, a Mr Clarke of Warwick, in December 1874. The building work was supervised by Colonel Grain, Commander Royal Engineers South Wales District, and by Colonel Hawthorne, RE. The estimated cost of the contract was around £65,000. The barracks were built to accommodate a sub-district brigade HQ, regimental depots for the 29th and 36th Regiments, HQs of the two militia battalions and staff and mobilization stores. Taking only three years to complete, by May 1877 work on the new barracks had been finished and the site was ready to be handed over to the regiment.

The construction of the barracks followed the pattern of the time and consisted of a gatehouse 'Keep', with offices to one side and officers' quarters to the other. There were two large barrack blocks, a cookhouse, two married quarters' blocks and a hospital. The area was enclosed by a 10-foot high wall.

Underneath the entrance to the Keep, a large water tank capable of holding some 20,000 gallons of water was installed, the water being supplied by the City of Worcester. Water from this tank was pumped by steam power into two cast iron tanks at the top of the Keep from which to supply the whole barracks. The remaining space within the Keep was used for storage.

The parade ground was located in the centre of the barracks with administrative buildings arranged adjacent to it. An office block was built for the District Commander's HQ, the Worcestershire Militia Battalion and Company HQs, and for Engineers, the Paymaster, and the Depot Companies of the 29th and 36th Foot. At the end of the office block were the Sergeants' Mess, the men's canteen and a reading room. The officers' quarters block provided accommodation for the Quartermaster, an Officers' Mess and accommodation for single officers.

The two barrack blocks for the men were two storeys high and consisted of four rooms, each built to accommodate 28 soldiers. A small room adjoining each barrack room was provided for an NCO. Behind the barrack blocks were the cookhouse and a bath-house. A drill shed for use in inclement weather was provided on the north side of the parade ground.

On the east side of the barracks two married quarters' blocks were built providing accommodation for 31 married men and their families. Behind the married quarters, a laundry with drying and ironing rooms was constructed for the use of the families. A primary school for the education of their children was also provided within the barracks. In the south-east corner of the site a hospital with beds for 28 patients, a surgery, an isolation ward and a hospital kitchen were built. Stables for the lodging of officers' horses, with straw and hay storage, were also provided on the site. To the north of the barracks and outside the perimeter wall nine acres of land was made available for military training and camping.

The front façade of the Barracks in 1880

Occupation of the Barracks

In November 1877 the 36th (Herefordshire) Regiment then stationed at Devonport were sent to Pembroke Dock, leaving behind 'I' and 'K' Companies, who were to form a combined depot with the 29th (Worcestershire) Regiment at Norton Barracks. These two companies under the command of Major G.P. Beamish arrived at Norton Barracks as the Depot Company of the 36th Foot, to prepare the barracks for occupation and to equip the buildings to scale, ensuring that all stores, equipment and accommodation were ready for the incoming personnel.[6] They were followed on 17 December 1877 by Captains G.W.F. Claremont and C.A.P. Cooper, Lieutenants F.C.H. Littledale and A.T. Ross, with Sergeant-Major T. Shattock, four sergeants, five corporals and 12 privates, under the command of Major R. Berkeley, who arrived as the nucleus Depot Company of the 29th Foot.[7] Having set out by train from Aldershot they arrived in Worcester, detrained and marched the three miles from the station to their new home.

On arrival the two Regimental Depot Companies remained entirely separate, each supporting their own regiment. To this end each Depot Company was allocated one of the large barrack blocks for the accommodation of their soldiers. The building assigned to the 29th Regiment was initially named Albermarle, but this was quickly changed to Farrington after the officer, Colonel Thomas Farrington, who had raised the regiment in 1694. The building allocated to the 36th Regiment was named Charlemont after Lord Charlemont, who had raised that regiment in 1701. On 19 December 1877 Lt-Col F.F. Hunter, of the 36th, was appointed the first regimental officer to command the new Sub-District Brigade.[8]

Early in 1878 the headquarters of the 1st and 2nd Militia Battalions moved from their depot in St George's Square, Worcester, to Norton Barracks where accommodation was found for their permanent staff. In April 1878 the War Office ordered the mobilization of the Militia Reserve and the First Class Army Reserve as a consequence of the fear of a war with Russia, and their staff was also quartered within the barracks.[9]

Lieutenant Colonel F.F. Hunter
Born in Bute on 12 May 1829, F.F. Hunter was commissioned into the 47th Foot in July 1848. He served with the regiment in the Ionian Islands, Malta, and Constantinople and in the Crimea, where he was involved in the Battle of Alma, the capture of Balaclava and the Battle of Inkerman. He was mentioned in Lord Raglan's dispatches for his part in the taking of the Quarries, a strong Russian position captured on 7 June 1855 and then held against repeated Russian counter-attacks, during which he was slightly wounded. He was present throughout the whole of the siege of Sevastopol, including the attack on the fortifications of the Great Redan, and the eventual fall of the city. He later served again in Malta and in Gibraltar, the UK and Canada. He joined the 36th Foot as a Major in June 1862 serving at the Curragh and Dublin before embarking for the East Indies in August 1863.[10] After further service in India he assumed command of the regiment in April 1870.[11] The regiment returned to England in December 1875. Having been on leave for most of 1877 pending retirement, he retired on half pay in December 1877. He was immediately appointed to command 22 Brigade Depot on its formation at the newly opened Norton Barracks, the first officer to command the depot and later 29 Regimental District Brigade. Colonel Hunter relinquished his command in December 1882. He retired as a Major-General in 1885 and died at the age of 57 in 1887. He is commemorated by a brass tablet, erected by his brother officers and friends, located in the north aisle of Worcester Cathedral.[12]

Initially all regular soldiers recruited into the Army in Worcestershire were sent to Norton Barracks. Those who had enlisted into other regiments or corps were, after a few days, given railway warrants to their own depots; those enlisted into the 29th or 36th Regiments remained at Norton for an indeterminate period of up to six weeks before being sent to whichever of the two regiments was based at home, where they underwent further training.

The initial training of regular recruits commenced at once,[13] and this was quickly followed by the training of militia personnel. On 8 July 1878, men of the 1st and 2nd Militia Battalions assembled under Colonel Norbury for their annual training at Norton and were accommodated under canvas on ground adjoining the barracks.[14] Training of militia recruits, which consisted of 55 days preliminary drill, was carried out at the barracks continuously throughout the year under the supervision of their permanent staff instructors. From 1878 the two Militia Battalions carried out their annual training at Norton while under canvas on the training ground opposite the barracks, and used the rifle range at Rainbow Hill for shooting.

Effect of the Childers Reforms
Under the Childers Army reforms of 1881, Hugh Childers, Secretary of State for War between 1880 and 1882, introduced further reforms which were essentially an extension of the earlier Cardwell reforms, under which the British Army was reorganised

2nd Militia Battalion officers in camp on the training field (1878)
Standing back L to R: Lt-Col M.E. Vale, Major W.P. Howell, Capt. J.S. Kersteman,
Lt M.H. Berkeley, Capt. W.H. Allsop, Lt J.V. Colby, Lt R. Holden,
Capt. H. Chillingsworth, Lt W.S. Clarke
Seated front L to R: 2/Lt M.R. Stubbs, unknown, Capt. T. Sheddon,
Capt. O.C. Walcott, Capt. H.W. Domville

into county associated regiments. The 29th and 36th Regiments of Foot became the 1st and 2nd Battalions of the Worcestershire Regiment respectively, with Norton Barracks as their Regimental Depot. The 1st and 2nd Militia Battalions became the 3rd and 4th (Militia) Battalions, The Worcestershire Regiment. The two Administrative Battalions of the Volunteer Corps became the 1st and 2nd Volunteer Battalions, the Worcestershire Regiment.

The new barracks, as well as providing accommodation and training facilities was also used throughout its history as a venue for the special events that regularly occur in the life of an infantry regiment. VIP visits, inspections and, in particular, the awarding and parading of regimental colours are examples of such activities. In December 1884, on a visit to Worcester by the Prince and Princess of Wales, the Regimental Band and a detachment from the barracks furnished a guard of honour at Shrub Hill Station, while a strong detachment of recruits lined the royal route. Another such event occurred on 28 June 1886 when the Countess Beauchamp, wife of the Lord Lieutenant of the county, presented new colours to the 3rd Militia Battalion during a parade at the barracks. The old colours were later deposited with some ceremony in the cathedral on 4 August 1887 in the presence of Field Marshal HRH The Duke of Cambridge, prior to his grand review of the armed forces of the county on Pitchcroft, to celebrate Queen Victoria's Golden Jubilee.[15]

Countess Beauchamp presents new colours to the 3rd Militia Battalion on 28 June 1886

2 THE BOER WAR TO THE START OF THE FIRST WORLD WAR, 1899-1914

In 1899 war broke out between Great Britain and the Dutch Republics in South Africa. As a result recruitment into the British Army increased considerably as men responded to the call to arms. As the war progressed the requirement for new recruits continued to rise in order to replenish the battalions fighting in South Africa. Such was the demand that the war strained to the utmost the resources of the British Empire.[1] In an attempt to alleviate the problem the Worcestershire Regiment, along with several other regiments, was ordered to raise two new regular battalions. This required a further change in battalion numbering. The two new battalions were numbered the 3rd and 4th Battalions, and the two Militia Battalions were renumbered as the 5th and 6th Militia Battalions.

During the war the depot acted as a mobilisation centre for the regiment as well as performing its usual role as a recruiting and training establishment. The barracks were on occasion sparsely occupied as, on completion of initial training, men were continually sent to home-based battalions to complete their training before joining drafts to battalions serving overseas. At other times, due to the large number of recruits under training and particularly on the raising of the two new battalions, the depot frequently became extremely short of accommodation. At a cost of about £50,000 two new accommodation blocks were built behind the two existing barrack blocks. The rooms were much smaller than in the two original buildings, each room accommodating ten men. These new blocks were later named the Higginson and Jacob blocks after two distinguished colonels of the regiment. At the same time additional and much needed facilities were provided when a mobilisation store, a gymnasium and a Sergeants' Mess were built on the north side of the parade ground.

Thomas Edward Galley, employed in a carpet factory at Kidderminster in 1900, had a strong desire to join the Army. He enlisted on 22 February 1900 and was sent to Norton Barracks on the same day:

> Arriving at the barracks, Norton some three miles from the City of Worcester, I was given my first army meal, four blankets and told to sleep on the floor and

The Barracks (1929) showing the Boer War additions.
The new accommodation blocks (Higginson and Jacob) are the long low buildings shown at the bottom of the picture (above the open field). The new Sergeants' Mess is located near the bottom left corner of the cricket ground behind the tree line.

manage the best way I could for the night. This came rather hard to me after leaving a good home; still I was determined to let nothing daunt me once I had enlisted. I was roused for breakfast next morning and told I should be for Doctor's inspection later on. I passed the doctor alright and was sworn in again enlisting for seven years with the Colours, five years on the reserve.[2]

As well as the recall of regular reservists and the induction of recruits, the depot staff had to contend with the mobilisation of the two militia battalions. Both the 5th and 6th Battalions volunteered for service in South Africa. They were mobilised for permanent duty in May 1900 and were based at Aldershot until October when they were stood down. The 6th Battalion was again mobilised in December 1901 and was accompanied by both its own and the Depot Band on its march to Norton Station where it entrained for Aldershot. It served in South Africa from January to September 1902. The battalion was entertained to dinner at Norton Barracks on its return.

In 1901 a fund was started to build two regimental cottages at Norton Barracks as part of the county memorial to the officers and men of the regiment who lost their lives

A view of the Regimental Cottages showing the Regimental Badge

during the South African War. A site close to the barracks was purchased in 1905 and building began. At a ceremony on 23 April 1906 the cottages were officially opened by Lord Coventry, Lord Lieutenant of the county. Built to house members of the regiment, the cottages' first occupants were Privates Price and Giles, both of whom had been severely wounded in action in South Africa and invalided from the service. Members of the regiment continued to occupy the cottages into the 1980s.

In 1908, following the formation of the Territorial Force, a further change in establishment saw the two Volunteer Battalions again renumbered, becoming the 7th and 8th Battalions of the Territorial Force, with their HQs in Kidderminster and Worcester respectively. The 5th and 6th (Militia) Battalions then became Special Reserve Battalions. (Special Reservists enlisted for six years and were liable for call up in the event of war. They initially did six months full-time training with a requirement to undertake three to four weeks training per year after that.) The depot continued to provide regular and militia battalions with trained soldiers and to hold the mobilisation stores for all reservists.

A small nucleus of regular officers and NCOs formed the permanent staff of the two Special Reserve Battalions. They were responsible for training the Special Reserve recruits so that, when the need came, they would be fit to fill the depleted ranks of the regular battalions. Recruits came into the depot to be trained for six months alongside recruits from the regular battalions, and each summer the reserve battalions were assembled for annual training. Camps were usually held in locations selected by the General Staff as likely stations for the battalions in case of war. In 1914 the 5th Battalion, by permission of the Earl of Coventry, were camped on his estate at Croome Park – the last occasion on which any battalion of the regiment was destined to wear the 'time honoured' scarlet of the 'old army'. On 4 August 1914, just prior to the beginning of the First World War, the Lord Lieutenant presented new colours to this battalion, the senior battalion of the old Worcester Militia.[3]

3   THE FIRST WORLD WAR, 1914-18

On the outbreak of the First World War and in response to a call for volunteers, tens of thousands of men enlisted nationally to swell the ranks of 'Kitchener's Army' (named after Field Marshal Lord Kitchener, Minister for War). Military barracks throughout the country were soon swarming with men, reservists and volunteer recruits, eager to join the fight in a war which it was thought, 'would be over by Christmas'.

In early August 1914 all ranks of the 2nd and 3rd Battalions, then based at Aldershot and Tidworth, were busy preparing for war. Battalions in general were short of men and had to be brought up to strength by the calling up of reservists. Depot staff at Norton Barracks had to ensure that reservists were properly prepared prior to joining their respective battalions. Stores of all kinds were obtained and taken into use. Among a multitude of preparatory tasks, all officers and men had to be medically examined and passed fit for war service. Regimental property was to be placed into safekeeping for the duration of the war and most importantly of all, the colours of the two battalions, the symbols of their history and loyalty, had to be laid-up. The escorts handed them ceremoniously into the care of the Dean and Chapter at Worcester Cathedral to be held until they were once again needed by the battalions.[1] Later, on 24 October 1914, the colours of the 1st Battalion were also laid-up in a crowded cathedral,[2] after the battalion's return from Egypt and prior to sailing for France on 5 November 1914.

Thomas Edward Galley, having served his seven years,[3] was one of the reservists called up. He wrote:

> The morning of August 4th 1914 broke finding me still on the reserve having recently joined for an extension on Section B Army Reserve. The General Order being issued and the Royal Proclamation being posted up calling all reservists to the Colours, I reported once more to Norton Barracks to await orders. Reserves started to pour in by the hundreds: many were the meetings of old chums, many were the handshakes. All sorts of rumours were going the rounds of the barracks, some very amusing, one to the effect that Germany had decided to withdraw having had notice of our declaration of war on her. Life at the barracks at this time was none too rosy. Men were coming in night and day by the hundreds and

the staff at the depot was much too small to deal with all the newcomers, not enough food was obtainable, not sufficient bedding, not enough washing accommodation, these were three of the main things that were lacking. This could easily have been avoided if they had called up the reserves in their proper order as they wanted them instead of having them called up all at once when they had no use for them. However 3 days at Norton Barracks saw me marked down for a draft to proceed for Devonport. Here I stayed for a short time eventually proceeding with a draft to France to join that small contemptible force known as the BEF.[4]

The depot having mobilised and prepared the reservists then sent them to bolster the ranks of the 2nd and 3rd Battalions, soon to be en route to France. Meanwhile the 5th and 6th Battalions were also mobilised, their reservists being assembled and equipped at the barracks before moving to their war locations near Plymouth. There they were responsible for completing the training of newly commissioned officers and men, and of those who had recovered from sickness or wounds and were due to return to the front.

The outbreak of war had caused a great wave of patriotic feeling among the British public and as men rushed to enlist, recruiting offices throughout the country were filled with willing volunteers. There were scenes of great enthusiasm at Worcester whenever the drafts of reservists and volunteers left the depot to fill the ranks of the regular battalions. Meanwhile the 7th and 8th Territorial Battalions had moved to the east coast to

Civilian to soldier; men undergo uniform fitting at the barracks during the First World War

Colonel C.M. Edwards, Depot Commander 1914 to December 1916

their war stations in Suffolk and Essex. As recruits flocked to join the county regiment, the depot at Norton became overcrowded and many had to sleep rough on the cricket ground and in the fields adjoining the barracks.[5]

The depot staff were under the command of Col C.M. Edwards who had returned from reserve service at the outbreak of the war and was assisted by several other retired officers, notably Major J. Chichester and Major G. Sandham.[6] They were strained to the limit by severely restricted training facilities, the great numbers of recruits to be cared for and an acute lack of accommodation.

Pte W. Barley arrived at Norton Barracks in August 1914 and recalled the conditions in the few days he spent there:

> After examination at Redditch we proceeded to Worcester, Norton Barracks where we found thousands of men waiting to be transported to the different depots. There we stayed until September 7th. I thought I should never forget those five days of hardships, as we thought, little thinking we should have to endure far more hardships than that. The barracks were overcrowded so we had no sleeping accommodation. I remember the first night, we were tired after standing up for a few hours, we were lucky if we could get one blanket each as it was very cold [at] night, it was not very pleasant to sleep out in the open with one blanket. We had a couple of footballs – some were playing football most of the night, to keep ourselves warm. The food was very bad, usually I think a piece of bread and marmalade.[7]

In 1915 the barracks played a crucial role in the development of what was then new and leading edge technology, when it was chosen as the Army's base for wireless training. The Royal Engineers set up the Wireless Training Centre Worcester (WTC)[8] at Norton Barracks, with local outposts including stables at St Martin's Gate and an interception station at Diglis. Selected soldiers undertook thorough training courses in wireless and Morse code before qualifying as wireless operators. The unit became crucially important to the war effort. The WTC was one of a very few training facilities in the country for Army wireless operators. (Other wireless schools existed to train operators for the Royal Flying Corps and the Royal Navy, including the Royal Naval Air Service. In addition many men were recruited from the General Post Office who had their own Training School.)

It is interesting to note that the wireless instructors at the barracks included men who were later to become leading figures in the field of British broadcasting and in other branches of science. Among them was the Adjutant of the WTC, the geologist Captain Raymond Priestley, RE. He had been a member of Ernest Shackleton's *Nimrod* expedition of 1907-09 and also of Captain Robert Falcon Scott's ill-fated

Royal Engineers Instructors, Wireless Training Centre, 1915

Terra Nova Antarctic expedition of 1910-13, and was a holder of the rare Polar Medal. He joined the Royal Engineers on the outbreak of the First World War and later served in France, winning the MC. The WTC remained at Norton until 1917 after which it departed for a new location in Bedfordshire. By the time it left Worcester its by now substantial strength numbered about 200 officers, 2,000 men and 200 horses.[9]

In 1958, when recording his time at Norton Barracks, Priestley wrote:

> We scoured the surrounding countryside on horseback and by car looking for sites for stations and billets for sections and established depots of several hundred men in the Worcesters barracks at Norton and at Malvern. Those years were too crowded for me to be able to recall a complete picture at this distance of time. We had in the summer a camp on Pitchcroft racecourse that housed several hundred men. We took over a dozen empty houses in town. I myself lived in lodgings at Commandery House in the centre of the town. 'Woodbine Willie' was a near neighbour to St Martins Gate and we used to see him on his rare leaves from France.[10]

Officers of the Royal Engineers Signal Service. Raymond Priestley is seated on the right. (Courtesy of Cadbury Research Library, University of Birmingham)

Continuing the association with wireless communication, the barracks was also selected to participate in early broadcasting experiments. This was the first instance of what became a recurring relationship between the depot, broadcasting and later, the BBC. In 1917 a handful of wireless pioneers – including Capt. P.P. Eckersley, who later became the first Chief Engineer at the BBC and Mr H. De A. Donisthorpe, a senior executive of the General Electric Company (GEC) – used primitive equipment to begin a broadcasting service to the troops at Norton Barracks from a tiny radio station at Diglis (Worcester). The programme, an early forerunner of Forces Favourites involving voice introduction to music and chat, was broadcast to an audience composed solely of military personnel. Because of that service, Worcester is officially recognised in vintage wireless circles as the home to the world's first ever public broadcasting station.[11]

As the war evolved and the demand for more men grew, new Service Battalions were formed to accommodate the continuing influx of volunteers and later on, conscripts. In November 1914, the 11th Battalion was quartered at Barbourne College Worcester (now Gheluvelt Park), but in early April 1915 they moved to Norton Barracks.[12] The 14th (Service) Battalion (Severn Valley Pioneers) were formed at Worcester on 10 September 1915 by Lt-Col H. Webb, MP and adopted by the War Office in March 1916. They were raised and later carried out their initial training at the barracks prior to moving to Larkhill, Salisbury Plain and later to Codford to complete their training, before embarking for France. They landed at Le Havre on 21 June 1916 and were subsequently attached to the 63rd (Royal Naval) Division.[13]

Depot staff continued to administer recruits throughout the war and thousands of men passed through the barracks prior to joining special battalions to complete their training before joining regiments at the front. As well as the time-honoured practice of 'drill' – used to instil a sense of discipline and pride – training in the use of weapons,

Recruits training in practice trenches at Norton Barracks, May 1915

field-craft, physical fitness and trench warfare formed part of the syllabus undertaken. What was in effect a civilian army was quickly transformed into an efficient body of fighting men, many of whom were to pay the ultimate price on the battlefield.

In addition to conducting infantry training the depot staff had to discharge many other duties, including providing guards for Austrian prisoners of war at a POW camp located just outside Worcester. Towards the end of the war the influenza pandemic which was responsible for the death of many millions of people throughout Europe killed a number of soldiers from the barracks and about 16 of the Austrian prisoners. Many of them were initially buried in Norton churchyard; in 1960 the Austrian soldiers were reburied in a German military cemetery near Birmingham.[14]

Officers and Senior NCOs of the Training Staff, 1918

4 THE DEPOT BETWEEN THE WARS, 1919-39

Immediately after the war and following the demobilization of tens of thousands of men, life at Norton became more relaxed. The early years between the two wars saw recruiting into the Army at a low level, understandably, following the appalling experiences of the First World War. Soldiering had, not for the first time, become very unpopular. Depot staff continued to train such recruits as there were, but a fair amount of leisure time enabled officers and men to participate fully in other aspects of county life and to pursue sport and leisure activities.

Lieutenant R. Newcomb recalls the leisurely approach to life at the depot during 1919:

> Other than the training of recruits, which for the most part was the job of the WOs and NCOs, there were good opportunities for recreation. I soon discovered this, when Malcolm [Captain M. Graham, his Company Commander] challenged me one day soon after I joined, after lunch in the Mess, and wanted to know why I was in uniform – and said 'unless there is something special on, we have lunch in mufti'. Life was good in those days. Two days of the week he was off hunting, and he encouraged his officers to ride and hunt. I enjoyed going out with him on one of the horses 'on the strength of the depot'.[1]

In 1922, as part of the overall reduction in the size of the British Army, the Worcestershire Regiment was reduced to two regular and two territorial battalions. The depot continued to produce trained recruits for the home battalions and also gave valuable assistance to all Officers Training Corps (OTCs) in the county and to Cheltenham College.

There has always been a diverse range of characters who have served at Norton Barracks. They include men known throughout the regiment for their special attributes, whether they were officers, non commissioned officers or private soldiers. There are men who have excelled on the field of battle, renowned for their bravery, its heroes such as Private Fred Dancox, VC. Others like Peter Richardson have stood out as leaders of men on the playing field, while Major Stacke, Colonel Everard and Colonel Lee are well known as regimental historians or administrators. Many men of strong personality have had the ability to lift the spirit of others in adversity, through humour or by example.

The depot was also not without its infamous characters. In December 1921 a young American born Irishman arrived at the barracks for recruit training.[2] Number 5245132 Private William Joyce had enlisted in the regiment. Joyce was to become notorious during the Second World War as Lord Haw Haw, broadcasting Nazi propaganda from his base in Hamburg. At the end of the war he was arrested and later brought to trial. Found guilty, he was convicted and executed for treason, having argued unsuccessfully that, despite still holding a British Passport, he had become a German citizen. The justification for his trial and execution remain a topic of fierce debate. His stay in the regiment was short-lived, as being underage for military service he was discharged in March 1922. Surprisingly, in view of his subsequent extreme right-wing activities, initially within the British Union of Fascists under Sir Oswald Moseley, during which he displayed extremely violent tendencies, and later in his support of Adolf Hitler, his character on discharge was assessed as 'Very Good'.[3]

As a consequence of the depression of the mid to late 1920s and 1930s, a time of mass unemployment, civil unrest and general strikes, many men once again turned to the Army as a way of making a living. Enlistment into all regiments began to increase and the now much smaller Army had a greater choice in its selection of men, so the depot staff saw an increasing number of new recruits arrive for training.

Depot Officers 1924, L to R: Capt. S. Parker, Capt. R.H.M. Lee, Lt E.C. Pepper, Major B.C.S. Clarke, Lt L.R. Tilling, Capt. M.A. Hamilton-Cox, Capt. G.S. de Courcy-Ireland

Many soldiers viewed recruit training as a necessary evil, something to be done and forgotten. Others were to find the experience both enjoyable and rewarding. Nearly all looked back on their time at Norton Barracks with pride at having achieved the high standard required of them to pass-out as fully trained soldiers. A large majority would say that despite the strict training regime, they would not have missed the experience. The diverse nature of the men recruited into the regiment and their experiences of life at Norton Barracks between the two world wars have been reflected by some in their memoirs. Their personal experiences provide a vivid picture of the hard times endured by many people during the depression and give an illuminating insight into the many reasons for which a man might join the Army.

Private Joe Sellars writes of his time as a recruit at the depot and extols the virtues of having a skill which could make life a little easier:

> Here I was in 1926, the year of the General Strike, 18 years of age and in a dead end job. My life was quite a happy one yet, on impulse, I decided to join the Army. As it was I enlisted into the Worcestershire Regiment at Dudley on 1st June, 1926; was given a railway warrant for the journey to Worcester from where I made my way to Norton Barracks. Captain Ford, the leading light of the cricket team discovered that I was a fair hand at the game and I was absolutely made when in my first game at Malvern and fielding at point I took four catches in one innings off his bowling. Thereafter I just couldn't go wrong, and had at least one half day off each week to play cricket.[4]

In 1927, a time of severe hardship for many, a very young Bert Phasey looked for a way to improve his life and decided that joining the Army was one way to do it. Many years later he wrote of his experiences and his reasons for choosing a military career:

> Let me take you back to the hard bleak years of the great depression to begin my reminiscences. It was then a common sight to see queues of young men lined up to see if they could be permitted to join the Army and on the 29th August 1927, at the age of 17 years I walked under the archway of Norton Barracks, Worcester. As I emerged into the weak sunlight, I saw before me stretched out, the barrack square. At that moment I took in old guns, a grass lawn and a motley collection of the lowest form of military misfits. The motley 'rookies' I found to be some of England's best, educated, clean and honest, they had joined in their hour of need. They gave of their unstinted best for their two shillings a day, a place to sleep and rough food. Gradually a warm glow of pride takes the place of former despair and total commitment stays with every member for every day of his life.[5]

Another new recruit recalls arriving at Norton Barracks in 1929 having taken the 'king's shilling'. His feelings must strike a note of familiarity with many who shared a similar moment:

Arriving at my destination at last, I spent some time standing in the roadway, not because I felt like admiring the architectural construction of the entrance, nor was I admiring the pastoral beauty of the surrounding country; in fact, I was endeavouring to persuade my knees that in order to support me in a fit and soldierly manner, they must stop knocking.[6]

George Dyer described himself as a bit of a dreamer and a rebel, whose waking moments were spent dreaming about the Army. Working at a lathe making nuts and bolts all day was not his idea of adventure so, in March 1932 after an argument with his foreman, George decided to join up. At the recruiting office a Grenadier Guards Sergeant invited him in:

'Now lad how old are you?' 'Sixteen', I replied. He sighed and said 'You don't want to join as a boy do you? Your pay will only be one shilling a day! Join as a man and it is two shillings. Here's two pence, go down to the coffee stall, come back and when I ask you how old you are, say eighteen.' And being naive, I did. Arriving at Norton Barracks we were met by a Corporal, he must have been six feet four inches tall [Corporal Tiny Rowbottam, MM]. 'What do you want sonnies?' I replied that we'd joined the Regiment! 'God help us', he replied. 'You poor little bastards, come with me I will find you a razor and you can go behind the gym and cut your throats.' I wondered what we were in for.[7]

Alf Deakin joined the Army in 1933 as a 17-year-old, to escape a job that he described as 'hard and boring', which was poorly paid and necessitated wearing greasy and oily overalls. Alf had a great deal of respect for the staff at the barracks and for the standard of training he received, but later recalled:

Like most recruits, at first I regretted ever having set foot in the place because of the very strenuous training and the stiff discipline. It certainly went against the grain with untamed youths like me. But most of the senior staff had been through grim times and graduated through a harsh initiation. They made sure in the curriculum set that we didn't get exactly mollycoddled. In six months they made boys into men.

Alf also recalled his dislike of Sunday Church Parades:

Recruits, if they were Church of England, had to parade for church service every Sunday morning. This meant spit and polish the day before to reach the impeccable standard demanded of us. There were two inspections, one by the squad Sgt outside the barrack block and the big one by an officer on the square. The inspection was followed by marching to the village church. The padre [Revd Verity] I think was a civilian. But he had a lot to do with the regiment because for a period I think he was editor of the Regimental Journal. He had a habit frequently of shouting during the service something like this. 'Don't get dozing off, those men in

20

the rear. Wake up and listen to the service. It will do you good!' These remarks were resented by many, including me. From then on I began to dislike Sunday church service including the spit and polish and the parading which preceded it.[8]

On Sunday 5 July 1936 the largest crowd ever seen at the depot was recorded, as nearly 16,000 people took the opportunity of attending an 'At Home' day, when the barracks were opened to the general public. Held to encourage and promote an interest in the Army, a series of events was arranged to entertain the crowds. Visitors were able to join conducted tours around the barracks, handle military equipment, try their skill on the miniature range or experience the gas chamber, using appropriate respirators, the supply of which proved unequal to the demand. The Regimental Museum was visited by 3,400 people (not including children) between 2pm and 8pm when the doors closed. Recruits showed their skill with training and PT displays, and the Training Company gave a demonstration of a King's Birthday Parade. The Regimental Band concluded with a concert under Bandmaster W.E.N. Sherratt.[9]

An important additional role undertaken by depot staff was that of taking responsibility for looking after regimental affairs, including regimental property, and maintaining regimental records and the extensive and historically important archives. Items including mess silver, paintings and other artefacts were cared for. They kept the members of the regiment informed by the production and distribution of the regimental magazine *FIRM*, in which articles covering regimental activities and news were

Depot Officers in 1937 ready for the hunt, L to R: Lt C.J. Myburgh,
Capt. J.J. Abbot, Major E.L.G. Lawrence, Capt. J.N.C. Chichester, Lt C.P. Vaughan

Major H.FitzM. Stacke, MC

Few men have left such a legacy of service to any regiment of the British Army as that left to the Worcestershire Regiment by Major 'Frank' Stacke, a brilliant and clever man.[10] As a soldier and military historian his contribution to his regiment can rarely have been equalled and certainly never surpassed. Frank Stacke was commissioned into the 1st Battalion of the Worcestershire Regiment from Sandhurst in October 1910. After service at Parkhurst on the Isle of Wight, he was posted with the battalion to Egypt in 1913. On the outbreak of the First World War he went with the battalion to France where he was severely wounded at the Battle of Neuve Chappelle in March 1915 and was repatriated to the UK. He returned to France in June 1917 and was severely wounded again during the storming of Langemarck; for his actions on that occasion he was awarded the Military Cross. Back in the UK he published his 'Notes on Regimental History' in 1917. In January 1918 he was attached to the Historical Section of the Committee for Imperial Defence where he was responsible for producing a compilation of the complete diary of the war. With Major H.T. Skinner he compiled a journal of the 'Principal Events of the War'. In July 1921 he returned to his regiment, joining the 2nd Battalion at Norton Barracks. He then applied his immense energy to his official duties and to a myriad of other matters. His involvement in establishing the Regimental Museum, his role as editor of the Regimental Magazine and his work as a regimental historian knew no bounds, and he put in considerable hours to achieve the accuracy and care for detail that characterised his work. His greatest work, published in 1928, was *The History of the Worcestershire Regiment in the Great War*, and was thought by many to be the best regimental history of the war to be written.[11] The excellence of his work led to the official historian, Brigadier-General Sir J.E. Edmunds, CB, CMG, asking him to write the history of the campaign in East Africa. He was given two and a half years' leave of absence from his regiment in which to do the work. Nearing completion and knowing that he was to proceed with the regiment to China, he applied all his energy to finishing the assignment. Towards the end of the task he was visibly tiring but rejected all appeals to spare himself. It was only his great spirit that kept him going and, completely worn out, he collapsed suddenly following a stroke. Major Frank Stacke died without regaining consciousness in the Millbank Military Hospital on 15 November 1935 at the age of 44.[12]

published. Another task taken on voluntarily by depot staff was to set up and develop the Regimental Museum and to care for and maintain the exhibits. The museum had been established in 1923 by Major H.FitzM. Stacke and was formed from a nucleus of badges and relics left to the Mess by Colonel H. Everard, a renowned collector and regimental historian. Major H.P.E. Pereira later improved and expanded the collection. Located initially in the Officers' Mess, it was moved to the Keep in 1935,[13] and from time to time to various other locations.

The International Crisis of September 1938 when Adolf Hitler's Germany threatened to go to war with Czechoslovakia over the Sudetenland, had a very marked effect upon the depot. Amid the fear of another world war, hurried preparations were made, lines of trenches were marked out near the married quarters and digging commenced. Steel shutters were erected and cellophane was pasted over windows to cut out lights in essential buildings. Every man, woman and child was rehearsed in his or her actions in the event of an emergency. Day and night practically ceased to have any meaning and then before all the precautionary measures could be completed, the emergency, to everyone's intense relief, was over.[14] The Munich agreement under which the Sudetenland was ceded to Germany only delayed Hitler's invasion of Czechoslovakia for a time. In exchange for British and French agreement, later denigrated as 'appeasement', a promise of 'Peace in Our Time' was signed by Hitler and British Prime Minister Neville Chamberlain. It was an agreement destined to fail: inside six months Germany had taken control of Czechoslovakia and within a year the world would be once again at war.

The Military Training Act of 1939 required all male British subjects of the ages of 20 and 21 resident in Great Britain on 3 June 1939, to register for military training. Having passed a medical board, they were enlisted as militiamen and were liable to be called up in batches for training from 1 July 1939, and at intervals of two months thereafter. The first batch of conscripts was sent to Norton Barracks in July 1939 and among them was Fred Mulley who, in 1976, was to become Secretary of State for Defence:

> Because of the novelty of conscription in England, we of the First Militia were given a good deal of publicity, and those of us who were fortunate enough, as we afterwards discovered, to go to The Depot, Worcestershire Regiment, were welcomed with considerable interest. I was very impressed by the great trouble our instructors, and indeed all the depot staff, took on our behalf, and the very friendly spirit we met right from the start. The list of those of us who have been fortunate enough to achieve promotion is too big to give, and is, I think, a fine testimonial to our depot training.[15]

The influx of new recruits into the depot, including the arrival of 150 'new militiamen',[16] required a large increase in instructional personnel and the appointment of additional support staff. The instructional staff came primarily from the existing battalions,[17] while many of the support posts were filled by members of a new organisation, the 40th (Worcestershire) Company, Women's Auxiliary Territorial Services (WATS), later the ATS. To prepare them for service all members of the company had, by July 1939 and prior to their employment at the barracks, paid a one day visit to the depot to see how the Army worked and to determine what their duties would be. This was followed by small parties of the company attending the barracks for 15 days 'in camp training'.[18] Their arrival at the barracks predictably attracted a great deal of interest, as one member of the Sergeants' Mess noted:

> The WATS were understandably the centre of attraction for some time when they arrived for their training, some of it carried out in the Orderly Room and some in the cookhouse and some in the Mess itself. Then the blow fell – the WATS were issued with uniform and all female allure fled in the face of the drab jacket and skirt. They became one of us, and from what little we have seen of them they will carry on the good work with fine spirit.[19]

After their training the ATS girls were very keen to get to work and just before 1pm on 2 September 1939, one day before Britain declared war on Germany, orders finally came for the company to report to the barracks for duty. Within one hour the ATS began to take up work in their allocated departments:

> It was a red letter day for the Company, as at last, they felt they were really getting down to business, and in a short time the cookhouse, Officers' and Sergeants' Mess kitchens and various stores resounded to the unusual sound of female chatter and laughter. The Company was soon detailed to its posts; the clerks to their various offices and the store women to the Quartermaster, Recruit, Mobilization, Depot and Sports stores. The cooks were making themselves at home in the more domestic tasks required of them in the Officers' and Sergeants' Mess and the cookhouse, assisted by the orderlies in the dining rooms.[20]

40th (Worcestershire) Company, Women's Auxiliary Territorial Service, April 1940

5 THE SECOND WORLD WAR, 1939-45

The tense political situation in Europe in 1939 and the subsequent invasion of Poland by Germany resulted in Britain once more going to war. Norton Barracks found itself again at the forefront of preparing soldiers for battle, and arguably began the busiest period in its history. The function of the depot – to train recruits and manage the regimental home – remained the same.[1] It also retained the responsibility of administering reservists. On call up reservists were processed and 'kitted out' at the barracks prior to posting to a battalion.

As well as managing hundreds of reservists, the staff at Norton had to train the other recruits, volunteers and conscripts from scratch. The number of men requiring training was such that a new training organisation was necessary to meet the increased demand. Initially the depot had become an 'Other Ranks Training Unit', carrying out initial training of men for many other regiments in addition to those of the Worcestershire Regiment. Recruit training was divided into Primary Training (first six weeks) and Advanced Infantry Training.[2] In September 1939 an Infantry Training Centre (No. 23 ITC) was set up at the barracks with two Primary Training Companies and two Corps Training Companies. It was formed from the staff of the depot and was commanded initially by Lt-Col J.F. Leman and then in October 1939 by Major (later Lt-Col) R.H.M. Lee. The depot staff, having discharged the responsibility for training to the ITC, were reduced in strength to four officers and a few other ranks who continued to look after regimental interests.

George Dyer, having 'served his time' and by then resettled as a civilian, remembers being recalled to service very soon after his discharge:

> I returned from India to Norton Barracks in April 1939, having completed my seven years with the colours. I had worked for two months when I received my recall to the colours. Arriving at the depot I found I was one of about five or six hundred, some having been on reserve for almost five years, others like myself having only just been discharged. We now saw the results of all the work put in by the quartermaster's staff, complete kits were waiting for us although those who had put on or lost weight had difficulties with their uniforms.[3]

Sam Beard was not impressed when in 1939 he arrived at Norton Barracks as a raw recruit:

> The red brick buildings and towered Keep of Norton Barracks rose ominously above us. At the arched entrance the sight of the 'magnificently bulled up' sentry made us feel like tramps. The massive Provost Sergeant, Sergeant Leatherbarrow did not need to say anything; the look of total contempt in his eyes conveyed his thoughts. We were allocated tented billets that were to prove totally unsuitable for the terrible winter of 1939. Three six foot planks supported on six inch trestles were to form the bed. We were issued with a coffin shaped palliasse and an empty bolster made out of a tough canvas material. The latter we had to stuff with straw before we could use it, there was no cover for the blue and white pillow. All the items had probably lain in the 'mob' store [Mobilization Store] since 1918. The drastic change in living conditions took its toll, seven hundred men reported sick on one morning. How many were genuinely ill, and how many simply wished to make a silent protest against the conditions will never be known. All efforts to protect ourselves from the severely cold weather came to nought.[4]

At the outbreak of the war, the numbers of men arriving at the barracks were so great that not enough accommodation was available to house them all, just as in the First World War. To ease the problem the old jam factory (later Morgan Crucible), located on the outskirts of Norton village, was requisitioned and tents were erected temporarily at the barracks to provide some badly needed if not wholly suitable dwellings. Short breaks away from the barracks enabled officers and men to find some relief from the difficult conditions. 2/Lt A. Maycock wrote:

> One of the pleasantest times was when we went with our platoon for a week at a time to a small country house Wheatfield (in Callow End) for a course run by Lieutenant Harris. The men were billeted in the stable block and we had rooms in the main house. The house had a powerful and inexplicable atmosphere. Most days we trained in and around the grounds of Madresfield Court. Anyhow the weather was marvellous and bread and cheese and beer at the local pub gave it all a holiday character.[5]

In 1940 major improvements in accommodation and in other essential facilities were provided when land around the barracks was acquired and a new hutted camp built. New buildings included large Officers' and Sergeants' Messes, a Junior Ranks club, accommodation blocks, two cookhouses, three parade grounds, MT garages and a NAAFI shop.

In addition to carrying out their primary role of recruit training, the ITC staff were required to undertake a number of additional war-related activities, as well as some that were unrelated to the war. Security, amid rumours of invasion, was paramount and in association with the Local Defence Volunteers (later the Home Guard) and the

Aerial view showing part of the Second World War development.
All of the buildings below the accommodation blocks and either side of the central parade
ground at the bottom of the picture are Second World War additions. A substantial part of
the new build (not shown) was located to the right of the road opposite the Keep.

other emergency services, ITC staff organised a number of joint exercises, including one to test the efficiency of a road block on the bridge on the Bromyard road. Number 3 Mobile Column from the ITC had the responsibility under the South Midlands Area Defence Scheme for the protection of aerodromes at Gloucester (Brockworth), Pershore, Worcester (Perdiswell), and Cheltenham (Staverton).[6] Other activities undertaken by ITC personnel included holding training days for the Worcestershire battalions of the Home Guard,[7] and acting as the enemy during Home Guard exercises. They also manned a radio post at the cathedral's tower, which was in communication with the barracks and a machine gun post on Whittington Tump. To support the local authorities, they also assisted in the unpleasant task of disposing of animal carcasses during an outbreak of foot and mouth disease.

Among the many tasks required in commanding a busy training establishment, the CO had to contend with a number of inspections and formal visits by the Princess Royal and senior figures from the services and the government. In 1939 the barracks welcomed one of many important visitors when the Right Honourable Leslie Hore-Belisha, the Secretary of State for War (who later introduced the Belisha Beacon and pedestrian crossings to British roads), arrived at the depot on a formal tour of the

The Right Honourable Leslie Hore-Belisha, Secretary of State for War, visiting in 1939. L to R: RSM A. Humphries, Earl Beauchamp, Major A.P. Watkins, MC, Right-Hon. L. Hore-Belisha, Major R.H.M. Lee, Major A.G. Little, Major-General F.C. Roberts, VC, DSO, OBE, MC

barracks, during which he was shown elements of the training programme and introduced to various members of the staff and trainees including the newly arrived ATS.

Exercises to test the readiness of local forces, military, civil defence, fire services or police were commonplace and could occur at any time of day or night. Even on a quiet sunny cricketing Sunday afternoon an exercise to test the reaction time of the ITC could be initiated:

> On the green in front of the Mess a cricket match is in progress. A figure is seen coming from the Orderly Room. It is the Assistant Adjutant. He strolls along swinging his cane whistling something which might be from *La Bohème*, but most probably is not. On reaching the duty drummer the whistle dies on his lips and, after a furtive look round, he whispers a few words. Then with a look of unconcern on his face, he continues towards the Mess. Meanwhile the Duty Drummer raises his bugle to his lips. The silvery notes ring out rising and falling in a call that is many years old and known to all men.
>
> The results are somewhat startling. The MT Officer, about to hit one of the bowlers for six, stays his bat in mid-air and receives the ball in the region of his belt. The PMC [President of the Mess Committee], who is umpiring drops four rounds of .38 and four stones into the pocket of his white coat, and sets out at a steady double towards the Mess. He is joined in rapid succession by OC 'D' Company and OC 'City Watchers'. The MT Officer, who has not recovered from the effect of the cricket ball making contact with his mid-day pint of cider makes a poor fourth.[8]

On the night of 18 January 1940 a major tragedy at the barracks was only narrowly averted when one of the married quarter blocks was destroyed by fire. Eleven families were affected, most of them losing all of their possessions. Mrs Edith Price remembers:[9]

We as a family lived on the top floor next to the Fuller family, in whose flat the fire started. My elder sister can remember us being picked up from our beds and taken down stairs to safety, just as the ceiling fell in, in our flat.

Between 26 May and 3 June 1940 the British Expeditionary Force in France was evacuated from Dunkirk under an action named Operation Dynamo. Thousands of British and allied troops were lifted from the beaches by an armada of large and small boats.

Troops were sent temporarily to barracks throughout Britain including to Norton Barracks. On arrival at Norton Station they were usually met by the remnants of the Regimental Band who played as they marched about a mile to the barracks. There they were fed, clothed, medically examined, paid, and sent on a week's leave with instructions to report to their own depots. Bereft of most of their kit, some items such as razor blades were in short supply. The CO, Lt-Col Lee, a man noted for his resourcefulness, immediately got the manager of the Worcester branch of Woolworths to open his shop and supply all he had, at the same time inviting a local bank manager to foot the bill. The feeling of defeat among the returning troops was quickly dispelled and many men were soon expressing a wish to return to the battlefield.[10] Brigadier Jack Smyth, VC, a First World War veteran, was one of those lifted from the beaches. He recalled his arrival at Dover and subsequent welcome at Norton Barracks:

I don't think any of us who made that journey back from Dunkirk will forget our arrival at Dover. The organisation there was superb. And everything possible was done to make the BEF feel that, although defeated, they had done their best. We found our train was bound for Worcester, where the Centre Commandant, Colonel Rupert Lee, was an old Dragon School friend of mine. He sent me straight to his house; a phone call was put through to Frances and within a few hours we were celebrating a reunion which neither of us had thought could ever happen again.

On Sunday 2 June Colonel Lee held a church parade at which he asked me to take the salute. I stood at the saluting base in the lovely old red brick triangle of the Depot of the Worcester Regiment while the troops marched past. Even in this short time they had cleaned and smartened themselves up, but they were a motley collection from every type of unit in the British Army. My arm raised at the salute began to feel like lead. And still more men came swinging past, over four thousand of them. Up to this moment I had no idea how tired I was. I felt very proud to have been privileged to take part in this great adventure with them; the very glorious disaster of Dunkirk which will be remembered as long as British history itself.[11]

Sam Beard, who along with others was moved out of his barrack room into civilian billets to make way for the men of the BEF, remembered the arrival of the Dunkirk veterans rather differently:

The first knowledge we at Norton gained of the Dunkirk saga was when some remnants of the British Army surged through the proud portals of Norton Barracks. They were dishevelled, dispirited, and wearing a variety of uniforms, even French ceremonial helmets. Their mood was defiant to the point of rebellion. Their reaction to a combination of neglected wounds, emotional problems and shock, was soon recognised by the regular soldiers at Norton as a likely catalyst for serious trouble. Despite being confined to barracks they broke out and painted the town [Worcester] red. Public houses hastily put up signs 'out of bounds to troops'. Following the breakout the full might of Norton's disciplinary procedure was exercised by the Commanding Officer, Officers, Warrant Officers, and Sergeants. However as the men were re-kitted and sent to their own units order was soon restored. Bearing in mind the trauma of Dunkirk and its effect on the men involved, the resulting order was a credit to the training and ability of the staff at Norton.[12]

Life at the wartime training depot fluctuated between periods of hard work and relaxation. Recreational and leisure activities were an essential component of recruit welfare in an otherwise strenuous war training programme and a regime of strict military discipline. These were provided in a number of different ways. Sports were popular; time spent at the cinema or relaxing in the NAAFI was hugely important, while the granting of an occasional 12 or 24 hour pass into town, or a trip home for those living locally, was eagerly awaited. In-house entertainment was arranged to improve the quality of the soldiers' spare time. Dances were organised and parties of local girls were bussed in from Worcester to provide welcome dancing partners. As far as the recruits were concerned, however, this was a complete waste of time because there were so many older soldiers that the young recruits hadn't a hope of finding a female partner.[13]

At a concert in July 1940 entertainment for the troops was arranged at the barracks, at which a varied programme of music, singing and comedy acts was provided by a party of Worcester and Kidderminster entertainers. Miss Queenie Main and her trio started the entertainment with a selection of favourite songs composed during the previous 50 years, in the choruses of which the troops joined wholeheartedly.[14] Other concerts were produced by the Entertainments National Service Association (ENSA), which was set up in 1939 to entertain the troops in every theatre of war. The ITC had formed an Amateur Dramatic Association and under the aegis of the Entertainments Officer, himself a well known professional actor and producer,[15] (having played with the famous British actors Charles Laughton and Henry Ainley at leading London theatres) staged its first production on Thursday 22 February 1940. The play, the comedy thriller *Someone at the Door* by Campbell and Dorothy Christie, was played to a very appreciative audience. The production boasted a star performer when the film and West End theatre actress Miss Jeanette Tregarthen provided professional polish in taking the leading lady role.[16]

Major J.D. Reynolds, destined to become the last Depot Commander, had been a member of Kings School Worcester OTC in the mid 1930s. When war broke out,

Colonel J.D. Reynolds, MC, MA

A member of Kings School (Worcester) OTC, where he was the Drum Major in the band, and therefore having worn the regimental badge since 1935,[17] John Reynolds enlisted as a private soldier in the Worcestershire Regiment at Norton Barracks in 1940. After training he volunteered for the Special Service Brigade and was posted to 3 Commando in Scotland. He took part in the Lofoten Islands raid in Norway during March 1941, and a raid on Vaagso, Norway in December 1941. Early in 1942 he was sent to 163 OCTU at Heysham (Lancs), was commissioned in July and posted to the 11th Battalion The Worcestershire Regiment. After spending a few months with the regiment he returned to 3 Commando, serving with them until the end of the war and winning his MC for operations in Italy between 27 August and 5 September 1943. After service in Germany, Canada and with the 1st Battalion in Jamaica he was appointed Adjutant to the 7th Battalion at Silver Street, Worcester in 1952 at which time he lived at Norton Barracks. He took command of the Regimental Depot in 1957, moving into Keren House adjoining the Keep with his wife and family. He was destined to become its last Commanding Officer and in 1959 had the painful task of overseeing the closure of Norton Barracks as an infantry training establishment. He later served as Assistant Adjutant General in Hong Kong and as Deputy Assistant Adjutant and Quartermaster General with the Aden Protectorate Levies. In May 1962 he was promoted to command the 4th Battalion The Cheshire Regiment (TA) in Chester, their first Regular CO. He also served with HQ Land Forces in Hong Kong and with the Kuwait Army before his retirement from the Regular Army. In 1972 he was appointed Commandant of the Worcestershire Army Cadet Force, and then of the Hereford and Worcester Army Cadet Force. He was later chosen to be the Honorary Colonel (1985-1990). In 1983 he volunteered for the job of Secretary for the Worcestershire Regiment Association, where he worked (very happily) until he was over the age of 70 when they said he had to give up![18] He was then voted in as President of the Commando Association for a year, and was then Vice-President until the Association ceased to exist in 2005. Since then John Reynolds has maintained close ties with the Regiment through the Regimental Association and the many events associated with Norton Barracks. In June 1995 he unveiled the new commemorative plaque on the Keep and in March 2011 commanded the Parade held to mark the closure of RHQ.

Lieutenant-Colonel R.H.M. Lee, OBE

Lt-Col Rupert Lee, born 6 April 1893, was commissioned from Sandhurst into the 3rd Battalion of the Worcestershire Regiment in January 1913. He embarked with the regiment for France on 14 August 1914 and served with them until wounded at Richebourg St Vaast in October 1914, after which he returned to England. He later served in Mesopotamia, India and England before returning to France, where he stayed until the end of the war. He was posted to the depot at Norton Barracks in 1924. Leaving the depot in November 1927 he subsequently served in India, Malta and China as well as in Plymouth and Aldershot. Promoted to Major in September 1934, he returned, succeeding Major E.L.G. Lawrence, to command the depot in November 1937. He remained as OC Regimental Depot until, on promotion to Lt-Col, he took command of the newly formed Infantry Training Centre (ITC). His tenure as CO therefore began at a critical time in the history of Norton Barracks.

Possessed of great administrative ability and an enquiring and inventive mind,[19] it fell to him to prepare the trainees, reservists and volunteers for war; in this he demanded absolute perfection from his staff, the trainees and himself. He showed great leadership in dealing with the influx of thousands of Dunkirk veterans and their inherent problems. In addition he worked tirelessly to meet the many demands made on him to work with the other local defence organisations. A man of diverse talents, he established the system of book-keeping for regimental accounts, had a great interest in photography and invented the 'Lee light' used for firing the Vickers machine gun by night. Relinquishing command of the ITC to Lt-Col S.A. Gabb in 1941 he was appointed Assistant Adjutant and Quartermaster General of the Central Midland Area from April 1941 and then as Assistant Quartermaster General Western Command from December 1941 until his retirement in 1944. In this latter role he played a major part in planning for Operation Overlord, the invasion of Europe, work for which he was awarded the OBE. On leaving Norton Barracks to take up his new appointment, an appreciation of Lt-Col Lee appeared in the January 1941 edition of *FIRM*:

> To this appointment there is an inevitable corollary: the I.T.C. has lost the services of its creator, of its most loyal officer, and – may I say? – servant. It must be said that no man is indispensable. But let it be said that, although no work of this kind can ever be called complete, the growth of the I.T.C. to its present stature is a thing well done – and it is the personal achievement of Lieutenant-Colonel Melville Lee.

Rupert Lee died suddenly at his home in Malta on 30 April 1975 at the age of 82.[20]

determined to join the Worcesters, and after completing first year exams at Oxford, he enlisted at the recruiting office in Angel Place, Worcester in July 1940. Told to report to Norton Barracks on 20 August 1940 he later observed:

> On arrival at the barracks I was amazed to see how much it had grown since my earlier visits; there were Nissen (or equivalent) Huts everywhere. I was put in a Potential Officers' Platoon in C Company, commanded by Capt. 'Gatsy' Garrett. We had an energetic time of training (about 8 weeks) – plenty of 'square bashing', route marches all around the area, bayonet practice on the specially-built course behind the 30yd range, and plenty of action in the gym. Every Friday afternoon all trainees were fell in on the main square, and marched past the CO by Companies; only if we did it well were we then allowed to get paid! We got 15 shillings a week, less any tax for barrack damages![21]

In 1941 a change of command took place when the Commanding Officer, Lt-Col R.H.M. Lee relinquished his command of the ITC to his successor, Lt-Col S.A. Gabb.

The staff of the South Staffordshire Training Centre, who had given up their own depot to an incoming American unit, arrived at Norton Barracks in July 1941. They joined the existing training establishment to form a combined infantry training unit within 23 ITC.[22] One of the responsibilities assumed by the joint ITC was to keep both regiments, wherever they were, updated and informed. This they did by compiling a monthly ITC news summary which detailed visitors to and events at the barracks, postings in and out, promotions and sports results, details of casualties and the award of decorations. The summary was distributed to units of the Worcestershire and South Staffordshire Regiments.

Continuing the depot's association with broadcasting, 24 May 1943 saw a famous county regiment and its regimental depot, the Worcestershire Regiment and Norton Barracks (unnamed at the time because of security restrictions), the subject of a BBC radio broadcast, in a programme entitled We Make Them Proud. Brigadier B.C.S. Clarke, DSO, gave an insight into something of the history of the regiment, proudly telling of the regimental museum and its treasures, describing life at the depot, of the valuable and splendid work undertaken by the ATS and how proud they were to serve. He went on to explain that the primary training programme undertaken was to prepare men of all branches and corps of the British Army.[23]

In 1997 Pte N.E. Carter recalled his six weeks primary training at the barracks:

> I enlisted at 29 PTC Norton Barracks in July 1943. The six weeks basic training included some of the weapons in use at the time. The Mark Five and Lee Enfield rifles, the Bren gun, Sten gun, Cup Grenade Discharger, the Vickers Machine gun and the PIAT [Projector Infantry Anti Tank]. Three fields adjacent to the barracks were at our disposal for field-craft, which included the [Whittington] Tump, that small hill which also served a purpose, for once one had arrived at the top the only way down was to hug one's rifle and roll to the bottom.[24]

German and Austrian prisoners held locally were assigned to carry out tasks around the area and within the barracks. Some were allocated to the Sergeants' Mess, where under the watchful eye of Sgt 'Curly' Dalloway they were given work, including being detailed to make habitable 'the cottage' for him and his family, following the fire in the married quarters:

> One of these prisoners was a very competent carpenter and made us wooden toys including a chicken on a board that was able to peck, and a beautiful swan rocking chair – how we wish we still had them.[25]

Although ready for war and doing more than their bit for the war effort, life for staff at the ITC was far removed from the danger and hardships experienced by men fighting on the world's battlefields, experiences which many of the training staff serving at the depot had themselves endured at one time. Young officers in particular found life there relatively comfortable.

Second Lieutenant A. Maycock, newly commissioned, was surprised to be told to report to Norton Barracks to join the Worcestershire Regiment, not his first or second choice, but something he never regretted. His memoirs are full of entertaining stories relating to life at the barracks:[26]

> Arriving at Worcester, I felt like a new boy at school with a mixture of pleasurable anticipation and some apprehension. Wearing gloves was a novelty, but the swagger stick had to wait arrival at Norton. The three or four months at the barracks were mostly very pleasurable. A gorgeous summer, relatively few duties and relaxed conditions enabling one to enjoy the companionship of the herd of young officers. Colonel Gabb was an ideal CO and Bob Durrant, the adjutant, friendly and approachable.
>
> The senior subaltern (a Lieutenant) looked like a personification of Bull, with his long twirling mustachios and arrogant air. We later heard about his nemesis in a copy of *Berrows Worcester Journal* which was sent out to India and he had certainly fiddled on a grand scale. The carrier platoon had done the harvesting on his nearby farm, his kennel man (he was joint master of the Croome hounds) came to the barracks once a fortnight to collect his pay, his four cars including a Rolls stretched the petrol rationing.
>
> We had two visits whilst I was at Norton, the first from The Princess Royal (King George V's daughter). About ten of us were receiving instruction on the Bren carrier. We were all crowded into the back of one driven by Harrap who had lost control. We understood that he had never previously ridden even a bicycle, but in any case, the steering or a track had jammed, and as we hurtled round and round in a circle, a side door opened and the Adjutant, sword erect and followed by the Princess and CO emerged. An hour later we were summoned by the stick orderly and lined up in front of the Adjutant where we were told our fortunes. Another visit was by the Colonel of the Regiment, Brigadier General Grogan, VC.

Frenzied orders were given for the photograph outside the mess; service dress, no sticks but gloves. As the Colonel approached, he was seen to be gloveless and there was a hurried and furtive removal of gloves and hiding them.

Every few weeks we had a party in the Mess to celebrate the departure of a draft. Particularly I remember a very large draft leaving for the 1st Battalion in Africa wearing their solar topees and led by the band as they marched down to the station. The next day they were back and there were several false starts, although not with the band, but the mess parties were repeated.[27]

Even in 1944 amid the lead up to D-Day and the invasion of Europe, life for the officers at Norton was not altogether demanding. 2/Lt B. Taylor recalls:

At the time I joined my unit as a Second Lieutenant in February 1944, life was still a 'bit of a game'. In the atmosphere of the Officers' Mess an inescapable nostalgia for the 1930s hung heavily in the air. The routine of an infantry depot Headquarters seemed steeped in the traditions of pre-war days. Colonel Gabb, the Commanding Officer, displayed a distinct ambience of India and the great days of the Raj, as he attended the weekly Dinner Night and, surrounded by the regimental silver, passed the port to his company commanders. The Victorian red brick barrack blocks added to the illusion; their archways and iron staircases encircled the parade ground and cricket field.[28]

On the 19 and 20 July 1944 a unique event occurred when, together with a large contingent of Staff and Regimental Officers, a formal meeting of the Colonels of the Worcestershire and South Staffordshire Regiments (joint administrators of 23 ITC), took place at Norton Barracks. Activities on the first day included a 'Saluting Parade' and Inter-Company sports meeting, while in the evening a Guest Night was held in the Officers' Mess. On the second day the event was rounded off with a luncheon accompanied by music played by the combined bands of the two regiments.

As the Second World War neared its end recruits continued to be trained under hard physical conditions and firm discipline. Ken Allen was called up in the last months of the war and on 18 April 1945 was sent to Norton Barracks to complete his basic training:

We were issued with blankets and introduced to our trainers, Sergeant Webb and a corporal whose name I can't recall. Following in the next few days were inoculations, a haircut, dental inspection, uniform alterations and swaps. The first night was the worst because everyone was feeling homesick, so much so that you could almost touch the feeling. When the lights went out we were alone with our thoughts and the silence was complete. I still hadn't got a clue, when my six weeks were at an end. My posting was given out at a parade, as were the others, by Sergeant Webb. I was heading for the Artillery Barracks at Deepcut. It was 'goodbye' to Norton Barracks. We'd been treated very well and neither Sergeant

Webb nor the Corporal ever used bad language. The food was good, and the char wasn't – but we drank it and never found out whether or not it had been doctored.[29]

Meeting of the Colonels: The Worcestershire and South Staffordshire Regiments 19 July 1944
Back Row, L to R: Lt F.B.T. Brady, 2/Lt Sanders, Lt F.B. Bate,
Lt N.G. Pepper, Capt. P.L. James, 2/Lt Harris, 2/Lt C.M. Saunders, Capt. J.F.A. Mervyn,
Capt. G.H. Duffield, MC, 2/Lt R. Watson, 2/Lt G.L. Hall, Lt C.A. Hexter-Stabbins,
Maj. D. Stevens, M.M.
Second Row: 2/Lt L.H. Raven, Capt. G.C. Reid, Lt J.D.M. Walker,
2/Lt L.W. Harrald, 2/Lt R. Lydiatt, 2/Lt W. Frith, 2/Lt K.G.L. Davies, 2/Lt B.C. Stanley,
Lt G.V. Sedgewick, Lt A.L. Vonetes (US Army), 2/Lt G.F. Howard-Smith,
Capt. F.A.C. Martin, Maj. A.T. Burlton, Maj. A.H.D. Wallace,
Seated: Maj. G.D. Baker, Maj. L. L'Estrange, TD, Revd J. Duffield, Capt. W. Waas,
Col A.H. Aldridge (US Army), Brig. G.W.St.G. Grogan, VC, CB, CMG, DSO,
Lt-Col F.G. Rogers, Maj. Gen. Sir G.de.C. Glover, KBE, CB, DSO, MC,
Lt-Col W.D.H. McCardie, Maj. D.C.N. McDonald, Maj. E.J. Harris, Maj. J.G. Player, TD,
In Front: Capt. W. Richards, Lt E.W. Leveratt, Capt. H. Johnson, Capt. E.C. Millington,
Lt H. Garrett, 2/Lt J.D. Vale.
(The Colonel of the South Staffordshire Regiment, Maj.-Gen. P.R.C. Commings,
CB, CMG, DSO, who was unable to attend, was represented
by Maj.-Gen. Sir G.de.C. Glover)

6   THE FINAL YEARS, 1945-59

In an effort to rationalise infantry training after the war, the training programme conducted at Norton Barracks was revised and in July 1946 the advanced infantry training element of the programme was moved to Oswestry.[1] A Primary Training Wing of two companies remained at Norton Barracks, administered for a time by No. 20 Holding Battalion. On the disbandment of 20 Holding Battalion in November 1946, No. 29 Primary Training Centre (PTC) was reformed under Lt-Col L.G.H. Bryant with the Primary Training wing of two companies, officered and staffed by the Worcestershire Regiment.

In the years following the war the depot once again began to enjoy a more leisurely way of life and had more time to receive and entertain visitors. The Reverend Frank Spackman, who had served as a corporal in the regiment before the First World War, visited Norton in 1947 and in his letter of thanks wrote:

> I cannot tell you how much I enjoyed the few hours at the Depot. The Regt is a family in a very real sense, and it was like a visit home. I also enjoyed my yarn with Sgt Lester. I am only sorry I missed Charlie Rose. In October 1913 I purchased my discharge in order to go out to the Mission Field. But I can honestly say that the day I walked out of the barracks in civilians was one of the most miserable days of my life.[2]

In July 1947 after nearly 250 years of unbroken service as the 36th Regiment of Foot and latterly the 2nd Battalion The Worcestershire Regiment, the 2nd Battalion was placed in 'suspended animation'.[3] As the battalion was never reformed it was effectively disbanded. A farewell parade took place on 16 July 1947 at Norton Barracks, held before a large gathering of past and current members of the regiment. A cadre of the 2nd Battalion commanded by Lt-Col F.S. Ramsay saw the battalion colours proudly handed over to the depot Commanding Officer Lt-Col L.G.H. Bryant for safe keeping in the Officers' Mess.[4] This was a particularly poignant event for those who had served in the battalion, none more so than Brigadier B.C.S. Clarke who had been the battalion's Adjutant at the Battle of Gheluvelt in 1914 and had commanded it with distinction in the 1930s.

Lt-Col F.S. Ramsay handing over the Regimental Colour of the 2nd Battalion to Lt-Col L.G.H. Bryant, Norton Barracks, July 1947

Colonel S.W. Jones

Colonel S.W. Jones was commissioned into the regiment in 1915 and was seriously wounded in France in 1916. He later served with the regiment in India, Malta, China and Palestine. During the Second World War he served in 1940 in France until evacuated at Dunkirk. He was later appointed to command a battalion of the Gloucestershire Regiment in India and retired from the Army in 1948 after which he joined the depot staff at Norton. Appointed as Administrative Officer, his role was to manage the museum and organise the regimental reunion as well as taking over editorship of *FIRM* from Major H.P.F. Pereira. He retired from the depot in 1960 and in 1961 moved to Devon where he died in 1962. Many members of the regiment attended his funeral in Tiverton.

Administrative changes in January 1948 saw the ITC move to Lichfield. Personnel having completed their primary training at Norton Barracks were then sent to complete their advanced infantry training at Lichfield. Then in April 1948 a decision was made that all Regular and National Service personnel would also undergo primary training at Lichfield and the PTC at Norton was disbanded.[5] The last parade of recruits passed out of Norton Barracks in April 1948.

With the demise of the PTC, Major J.H.A. Dean was appointed to command the depot, with a retired officer, Colonel S.W. Jones, as Administrative Officer. They were given a clear mandate as custodians of all regimental property and the responsibility for administering and maintaining their part of the barracks. New responsibilities were defined as: to act as headquarters of the regiment, to provide administrative facilities for Territorial and cadet training and to administer various categories of personnel.[6]

With such a small establishment, the depot staff could not be expected to take on the responsibility of caring for and maintaining the entire Norton Barracks site. Their responsibility was limited to their own accommodation which consisted of the two blocks either side of the Keep and the Keep itself, as well as Farrington block, which then housed the Regimental Museum, and Charlemont block. The remainder of the barracks was occupied by the 49th Anti-Tank Regiment Royal Artillery who arrived from Germany to take on the role of assisting the Territorial Army. They were one of many 'lodger' units who were to occupy the barracks at various times until its final closure.

In 1948 the Colonel of the regiment invited all retired officers, and expected serving officers, to subscribe a small sum annually towards a regimental officers' mess at the depot. The purpose of this was both to encourage retired officers to use the mess and to help fund the entertainment of key people in the county. This initiative had the effect of increasing the cohesion of the regiment by holding events involving both retired and serving officers, and providing the funds to bolster the regiment's profile in the county. On his retirement from the post of RQMS of the depot, Mr Frank Oldham was appointed to manage the mess.

On 15 April 1950 the regiment was honoured by the City of Worcester when it was presented with the 'Freedom of Entry' to the city and with a superb gift of a set of silver side drums. The parade, during which the colours of the 1st Battalion, the 2nd Battalion and the 7th Battalion were paraded, took place on the county cricket ground. The presentation to the regiment was made by the Mayor of Worcester, Alderman T.S. Bennett and was received by the Colonel of the regiment, Brigadier B.C.S. Clarke. In attendance were the previous Colonel, Brigadier G.W.St.G. Grogan, VC, and General Sir Richard Gale the Colonel designate of the Worcestershire Regiment. Following the presentation, the 1st Battalion, followed by comrades of the 1914-18 war and a large contingent from the 1939-45 war, marched through the city to a service at the cathedral which included the unveiling of the war memorial in the Chapel of St George. At the march-past at the Guildhall, the mayor took the salute with the Colonel of the Regiment and members of the council in attendance. The day was rounded off by a reunion at Norton Barracks, where many old friendships were renewed as over 1,500 people sat down to tea.[7]

In January 1951, amid much talk of re-armament, Norton Barracks welcomed the arrival of an advance party of American airmen, who took over the accommodation vacated in November 1950 by the 49th Field Regiment RA.[8] In a short ceremony on 30 January the American flag was raised for the first time alongside the British flag at the barracks. The ceremony was attended by Lt-Col E.D. Pearson, commanding the United States Air Force (Anti-Aircraft) Detachment, and his officers and men. The depot contingent consisted of the OC Major J.H.A. Dean, Capt. M.J. Ratcliff and RSM A. Foden. The Union Jack was raised by Master Sergeant R. Webb of the USAF and the Stars and Stripes by RSM A. Foden.[9] Mrs Edith Price recalled seeing the arrival of the Americans:

Regimental Quartermaster Sergeant (RQMS) F.S. Oldham, MSM

Born in Blackburn in July 1899, Frank served with the Kings (Liverpool) Regiment from June 1918 until November 1919. On 27 November 1919 he joined the 4th Battalion of The Worcestershire Regiment at Cologne. In 1922 he was posted to the 2nd Battalion in Dublin. He served in Germany, Plymouth and Malta. Then in 1934 he went with them to China and in 1936 to India. Posted to Home Establishment as a RQMS in 1938, he joined 23 ITC at Norton Barracks, an appointment he continued to hold until he completed his service in 1947. On discharge he continued to live at the barracks in what was known as 'Mr Oldham's house' (next door to the RSM) and was employed as caretaker and Mess Steward at the depot, later the Regimental Mess, an appointment he held until his death 19 years later. Having been a prominent member of the Sergeants' Mess, being involved in and organizing many of its activities, he later threw all his energy into the care and maintenance of the Regimental Mess. He knew personally almost every officer in the regiment, many of whom he had served under. His attention to detail during Cricket Week, the Boxing Day Hunt or garden parties and numerous other regimental and social events was legendary, and all who used the Regimental Mess owe him an immense debt of gratitude. Frank Oldham died suddenly of a heart attack at home in his regimental quarters on 16 December 1966 aged 67. He had served the regiment for almost the whole of his life and was 'still in harness' as he would have liked to be, at his passing. Frank was given a funeral with full military honours at Norton Church on 21 December, which was attended by, in addition to his family, a large number of past and present members of the regiment.

They trundled along Norton Road in their huge lorries, with gleaming white smiles beaming out of their transport, throwing out chewing gum/bubble gum to the children around and later providing NYLON stockings for the ladies and cigarettes for the men.[10]

In January 1952, less than four years after the last parade of post-war recruits had passed out of the depot, Norton Barracks once again took on the role of providing the basic training of recruits for the regiment. This followed the re-introduction of Regimental Depot Training by General Gale, then the Director-General of Military Training.

The Stars and Stripes flying alongside the Union Jack in 1951

From 1952 recruit intakes consisted mainly of National Servicemen with sometimes a few regular soldiers. Training initially lasted for six

General Sir R.N. Gale, officers and members of the Sergeants' Mess
upon the return of infantry training to the depot, 1952
Back Row, L to R: Sgt Lynch, unknown, unknown, Sgt Cushen, Sgt Bell, unknown, Sgt Platt
Centre Row: Mr Shaw, Mr Dalloway, Sgt Crompton, Sgt Cooper, Sgt Jones, unknown,
unknown, Drum Major Gay, BSM Morgan, unknown, Mr Oldham
Sitting: C/Sgt Sopp, RSM A. Foden, Major J.B. Brierley, Lt-Gen. Sir Richard Gale,
Lt Batchelar, Bandmaster Hayes, unknown

weeks but by 1953 had been extended to ten. Intakes of one or two platoons of about 28 men each arrived on a Thursday, drew their clothing, equipment and bedding from the Quartermaster's stores presided over by ex-RQMS W.S. 'Dinky' Shaw, loaded it all into their canvas mattress covers and carried or dragged it to their allotted barrack room.

Regimental Quartermaster Sergeant (RQMS) W.S. 'Dinky' Shaw

Dinky Shaw devoted a large part of his life to the Worcestershire Regiment, first as a soldier and afterwards as a civilian. Born in Dudley, he enlisted at Norton Barracks on 28 October 1925, joining the 2nd Battalion. Two years later in 1927 he was posted to the 1st Battalion at Allahabad in India and served with them in China, Plymouth and Aldershot until 1937 when, as a Sergeant, he was demobilized on completing 12 years' service. He was recalled in 1939 for service in the Second World War. Initially he served at the depot as a drill and weapons training instructor until in 1942 he was promoted to Warrant Officer Class II (WOII) and appointed Regimental Quartermaster Sergeant with the 7th Battalion (TA). He went with them to India and served with distinction in Burma, including the Battle of Kohima, and at Maram where he suffered a severe leg wound. This resulted in his being invalided home, and subsequently discharged in 1946. After demob he moved with his wife into No. 2 Regimental Cottages at Norton Barracks, where they lived for 35 years. He joined the Quartermaster's staff as a civilian clerk, a job he held until the formation of the Regimental Headquarters in 1959, when he was appointed as RHQ's first clerical officer, a post he held until he retired in 1972.

Dinky was another exceptional all round sportsman and athlete representing the battalion at football, cricket, hockey and athletics. He captained the battalion football team from 1929 to 1932 and played for the Army in 1935 and 1936. His other activities included being Treasurer of the Sergeants' Mess Reunion and Hon. Secretary of the 7th Battalion (T.A.) All Ranks Reunion in Kidderminster from 1961 to 1967. In 1963 he became the first Chairman of the Worcester Branch of the Worcestershire Regiments' Association, a post he held until 1971. He was held in deep affection and the highest regard by thousands who served in the regiment before, during and after the Second World War. Dinky died on 24 May 1982, his funeral being attended by a large gathering of ex members of the Worcestershire Regiment; the address was given by Colonel J.W.B. Stuart, MBE, MC.[11]

Corporals who were to act as the squad instructors were on hand throughout the first few days to guide, help and chivvy the newcomers to get organised. They marched them to the cookhouse for their meals, ensuring they took with them their knife, fork, spoon, tin mug and mess tins. The first three days were spent having haircuts and inoculations, marking all their clothes and equipment with their eight digit number, 'bulling' their boots, and learning how to assemble and blanco their webbing equipment, press creases into their battledress and lay out their kit for inspection in the prescribed manner.

They had to pack all their civilian clothes and send them home, and were not allowed out of barracks until they were judged smart enough to be seen in public in their uniform. The platoon sergeant normally appeared briefly in the barrack room on the first evening and the officer in charge of the intake gave them an introductory talk the following day. As soon as reveille sounded a fully dressed corporal appeared in the barrack room to ensure everyone got out of bed promptly. Each day beds had to be stripped and blankets and sheets folded neatly at the head of the bed.

Training by squad instructors started in earnest on the Monday of the first week following recruit induction and consisted of PT and drill by platoons with frequent inspections for turnout both on the drill square and in the barrack room, lessons on fieldcraft, the rifle, machine gun and later the sten gun, with regular breaks for a smoke. Once weapon handling and cleaning had been mastered recruits progressed to live firing on the 30-yard range. It was a strenuous regime and many found it hard to stay awake during the occasional lecture or training film.

After the first few days, when the initial shock was wearing off, the hard sell to convert two-year National Servicemen into regulars started. A National Serviceman's starting rate of daily pay was four shillings (20p) as compared with a three-year regular's

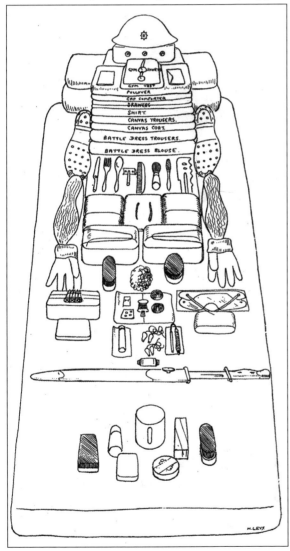

How kit had to be laid out on the bed when there was a kit inspection

seven shillings (35p). The platoon sergeants put blackboards up in the barrack rooms to demonstrate how much better off a regular was, and an added incentive for those who converted was a red lanyard to wear on their battledress. It was a temptation for many and quite a few succumbed. Though the weekly wage was 28 shillings, National Servicemen rarely received more than £1 on pay parade on a Thursday after deductions for haircuts and future possible barrack damages, on top of which there was blanco, boot polish and brasso to be bought. The last meal of the day was tea and the temptation to go to the NAAFI in the evening for a snack and a beer was strong.

Most men adapted well to the discipline and the training regime but occasionally somebody kicked against it. John Lowles recalled:

> A man named Bray in my recruit intake went absent within days of our arrival in September 1953 and, after being apprehended, subsequently escaped from detention regularly. On one occasion he was collected from the guardroom by Colour Sergeant Johnny Sopp to work in his stores. When Sopp unlocked the door the man pushed him inside, locked the door and absconded. Sopp was incarcerated in his store for some hours before someone heard him banging on the window and released him. Bray was still in detention when the rest of the intake completed their training.

Colour Sergeant J. Sopp

John Sopp enlisted in the Worcestershire Regiment in 1919. After having served in the UK, Malta, China and India he was posted to the Regimental Depot in 1939 and became a fixture, staying there for 17 years until his retirement in 1956. An excellent PT Instructor, he was also a fine games player; in his younger days he represented the 2nd Battalion at Hockey, a game at which he excelled. He was one of the best known personalities ever to serve in the regiment, with an exceptional ability in organising events or social functions such as the Annual Reunion and Sergeants' Mess dances.[12] Of unique character and fame, he had a legendary mystique in acquiring wholesome rations and many other commodities from sources only he knew about; this was often the subject of comment amongst the officers of the depot. The general consensus was that probing was undesirable and – such was his efficiency – unnecessary.[13] John was delighted to receive the 1937 Coronation Medal and was the first soldier in the regiment to be awarded a clasp to his Long Service and Good Conduct Medal. Johnny Sopp died on 1 January 1962 and after a funeral service at St Stephen's Church, Worcester attended by a host of former friends and colleagues, his ashes were buried in Norton churchyard.

The first milestone in the training took place at the end of the sixth week when the Adjutant inspected the intake on parade. If he was satisfied with their turnout and bearing the recruits were allowed out of barracks for the first time until midnight. The downside was that they then also became eligible for guard duties which involved periodically being inspected on mounting and dismounting guard and spending the night on guard for two hours on and four hours off.

By this time shooting, a high priority because of the regiment's strong reputation, was taking place at Tyddesley Wood firing ranges near Pershore; after shooting practice the recruits often marched the five or so miles back to barracks at a brisk pace. The shooting programme concluded with a test to determine each man's ability with the rifle and light machine gun. Those who attained the highest standard were awarded marksman's badges to wear on their battledress.

The intake normally spent a few days away on field training at a military training area before the last week when a final effort was made to perfect the drill for the passing-out parade. The big day dawned with the recruits cleaning their equipment and pressing their battledress before falling in on parade for inspection by a senior officer or local dignitary in front of their families. After the inspection, the best recruits at drill and shooting and the best recruit of the intake received merit certificates; from 1952 the latter was also awarded the cup presented by General

Following their passing-out parade Privates Bill Eckley and 'Tanky' Taylor proudly display their shooting qualification badge for the Light Machine Gun, c.1958

Gale. The Gale Cup was first presented on 11 February 1952 on the completion of the first initial six weeks basic training course, when Brigadier J. Gifford presented it to Private E. Smith of Ramillies Platoon. Private Smith later served in Malaya and went on to be one of the relatively few National Servicemen to rise to the rank of Sergeant. The parade finished with a march past as the recruits stuck out their chests and gave an 'Eyes Right' to the inspecting officer as their proud families watched. After the parade, they were free to go home with their families for a week's leave, or two if they were to be posted abroad, before returning briefly to be posted to the 1st Battalion, or sometimes to another regiment of the Mercian Brigade.

The Lord Lieutenant, Admiral Sir William George 'Bill' Tennant, KCB, CBE, MVO, DL, presents a merit certificate to a recruit during a passing-out parade. RSM A. Foden stands in attendance

Pte E. Smith, the first winner of the Gale Cup for best all round recruit

Philip Turner, a National Serviceman called up in January 1953, arrived at Norton Barracks to commence training:

> I became a member of Sgt Jones' Platoon.[14] The training and discipline was second to none as was the pride in the Regiment. I recall an occasion when the platoon was making one of its innumerable runs up Whittington Tump when Sgt Jones took hold of two rifles from two complaining recruits and proceeded to beat us all to the top. They were hard days but happy days shown by the fact that every one of the platoon contributed towards a gift for Fred Jones when the training was finally over.[15]

On the re-introduction of training the depot had once again assumed responsibility for holding and maintaining stores and kitting out

Inspection at a recruit passing-out parade in 1954.
L-R: Capt. C.E. Potts, RSM A. Foden, Major J.B. Brierley, Capt. Batchelar,
Sgt Jones, Capt. A.M. Gabb, General Sir Richard Gale.
The be-medalled recruit is Pte S. Adams who was surprised on re-enlisting to learn that,
despite serving during the Second World War, he had to undergo basic training.

reservists prior to posting. This continued in the old part of the barracks until 1959 when training at the depot once again came to an end and all training was again transferred to Lichfield.[16]

The Midland Home Service having broadcast a 30 minute programme on the history of the Worcestershire Regiment on 8 October 1948,[17] the BBC returned to the barracks in 1953 when the depot was used as a location for broadcasting another radio programme and a follow up television programme. The radio programme entitled 'We Make Em Proud', the title clearly based on the earlier broadcast of 1943, was transmitted on 27 March. It told the story of the British infantry and was based on the history of the 29th Regiment of Foot. Presented by the BBC's Philip Donnellan, 'it showed how the national serviceman who joins the regiment inherits a great tradition'. This was followed by a TV broadcast on 5 May 1953 entitled 'The Fighting Midlands', the rehearsals for which were hard work, that brought the story up to date.[18] Commentary was again by Philip Donnellan, while in front of the camera interviews were conducted by the famed BBC war reporter Chester Wilmot.[19] The Officer Commanding the depot, Major Brierley, was the primary performer for the depot and

*BBC reporter Chester Wilmot (hands in pocket) filming at the depot in 1953.
Major J.B. Brierley is facing the camera*

fielded most of the questions. All parts of the barracks were examined and the soldier's lifestyle and training programmes all came under close scrutiny. The opening sequence showed the Regimental Band marching under the Keep archway. The museum was featured with the BBC reporters enlightened by Colonel S.W. Jones. Recruits were filmed during physical training and weapon training, while labouring on the assault course and shooting on the firing range. The BBC also filmed the induction process, when, after undergoing documentation, new recruits, often bemused by it all, were subjected to military-style haircuts and medical examinations. Then, to show how recruits had developed after their training, the now smarter, wiser and fully trained soldier, proudly attending his passing-out parade, was faithfully recorded.

The year 1953 saw the coronation of Queen Elizabeth II. The regiment was heavily involved in local celebrations. A Coronation Party from 1st Battalion led by Major

The Coronation Colour Party, 1953

The Regimental Band performed many concerts during the Coronation celebrations

A.H. Nott and the 7th Battalion led by Major E.R.W. Tooby, who were to march in the Coronation procession in London, and a street-lining party led by Captain A.M. Gabb provided by the depot, for which there was keen competition for places, both carried out their training for the event at the barracks. Other local celebratory activities included a review by the Lord Lieutenant, Admiral Sir William Tennant, on Pitchcroft. The regiment was represented by a detachment of soldiers from the depot, the Regimental Band and a number of old comrades. The families at Norton Barracks took part in the festivities by joining the local Norton village celebrations.[20] The Regimental Band was in great demand during the Coronation celebrations and fulfilled numerous engagements across the county.[21]

From 1952 until 1956 Norton Camp, the hutted camp opposite the Barracks, was occupied by Number 6 Training Regiment Royal Engineers. Later Norton Barracks was occupied by many units either in transit or for longer periods in residence, including the 1st Battalion, the Worcestershire Regiment in late 1956 and the 1st Battalion, the Sherwood Foresters in 1959.

In April 1955 Mrs Dorothy Ricketts, wife of the Commanding Officer arrived to take up residence in Keren House, next to the Keep. Fifty years later in 2006 she recalled her time there:

> When I drove into Norton Barracks on a sunny April afternoon in 1955, National Service recruits were being drilled on the Parade Ground. Before my 5-year-old son and I went into what was then called the CO's house, we turned around and looked across the Green to the Sergeants' Mess. To our left were Charlemont and Farrington blocks, to our right were the homes of the other ranks' families. Next to them were the semi-detached houses of RSM Foden and Mr Oldham the Officers' Mess steward. Chestnut trees in full leaf marked the perimeter of the Cricket Green.[22]

No 2 (Gallipoli) Platoon, November 1954 - January 1955
Standing, L to R: Privates D. Key, G. Lawrence, B. Hubble, C. King, J. Linell, R. Omasta,
B. Grove, J. Farley, A. Allison, J. Tipping, R. Moore, W. Probert, J. Hill, H. Wall, J. Brain,
T. Chance, I. Dick, R. Watkins, D. Sedgewick, J. Basterfield, D. Portman, B. Sayers, R. Sloane
Seated: Cpl C. Hadley, Sgt G. Parkin, L/Cpl B. Gowan

The Corporals, 1955-56
Back row, L to R: unknown, L/Cpl Shepard, unknown, L/Cpl Hanson, L/Cpl Halford,
unknown, unknown, L/Cpl Dent, L/Cpl Durrant, unknown, unknown, L/Cpl Berkley.
Centre Row: Cpl Renfrew, Cpl Reay, Cpl Stokes, Cpl Sturrock, unknown, L/Cpl Hardiman,
Cpl Rushton, unknown, unknown, Cpl Layland, unknown, Cpl Harper, Cpl Beresford.
Front Row: Cpl Morris (82),[23] Cpl Harris, Cpl Moore, Cpl Hinsley, Capt. C.E. Potts, Major
J.D. Ricketts, RSM A. Foden, Cpl Dickens, Cpl Morris (52), Cpl Groves, Cpl Clarke

Her memories give an interesting insight into what was and had been since the opening of Norton Barracks, a typical regimental way of life, in particular in relation to both formal responsibilities and the importance of sporting events:

> Believe it or not, in 1955 the Depot CO and his wife were required to pay formal calls on the Lord Lieutenant, the Bishop of Worcester, the Dean of the Cathedral and the Mayor of Worcester. In June each year, cricket week took place and several matches were played at Norton Barracks as well as a two day match against the Worcestershire Gentlemen at the County Ground.[24]

For seven years recruit training was conducted at the depot. The routine of a regimental depot continued much as it always had, with training and sporting activities playing a major role in the life of staff and trainees. Many hundreds of National Servicemen passed through and had their first taste of Army life under the watchful eye of RSM A. Foden and the training staff. Their initial feelings were mellowed by the passing of the years and in spite of the tough training schedule many would say how much they enjoyed life at Norton Barracks. Unhappily it was not to last and in

Regimental Sergeant Major (RSM) A.C. Foden, MSM

RSM Albert Foden joined the regiment on 24 April 1930 and was to have a long military career, serving for over 36 years. He was an exceptional soldier and was destined to achieve rapid promotion to the highest non commissioned rank. Prior to the Second World War he served with the 2nd Battalion in India where, promoted to Sergeant in March 1938, he was known as an excellent Machine Gun Platoon Sergeant. During the war he was first seconded to the Indian Corps of Clerks and after the Normandy landings served in Belgium and Holland with the Canadian Division. After the war he took up an appointment within the War Office.

Albert Foden served as the Depot Regimental Sergeant Major at Norton Barracks from July 1948 until early 1957, an unusually long time to be in post. His tenure included most of the time during which the majority of young men in Britain were required to carry out compulsory National Service. On leaving Norton Barracks RSM Foden took up an Extra Regimental Employment (ERE) appointment at Beaconsfield. In 1956 he was awarded the Meritorious Service Medal (MSM) and in 1966 a clasp to his Long Service and Good Conduct Medal, one of only two recipients in the Worcestershire Regiment.[25] Following his retirement from the Army he helped as a volunteer with the work done by SSAFA in aiding service families. Albert Foden died quite suddenly at the age of 66. His funeral in Bath was attended by many of his old comrades.

1959 the decision was taken to once again relocate all infantry training to Lichfield. On 21 July 1959 the last ever passing-out parade on the square at Norton Barracks was staged. This was the passing-out parade of Kluang Platoon which consisted of six regular servicemen and 39 National Serviceman, ten of whom who would 'sign on' to become regulars the same day.[26] The parade was inspected by Brigadier D.H. Nott, who presented the Gale Cup to the best all round recruit and afterwards took the salute as the recruits marched past.

July 1959 also saw the closing of the depot as a training centre, and the training staff, including the last depot Regimental Sergeant Major, RSM T. Hands, moved to Lichfield. The depot administrative staff stayed on at Norton until 22 September 1959 when they too left.

Alec Mackie was a member of the rear party left behind to close down the regimental depot and clear out the barrack blocks. He wrote:

> It was during this clear out that a pile of sealed boxes was discovered 'hidden' under other equipment. Each box contained several hundred rounds of .9mm ammunition all of which was unaccounted for on any QM ledger. I know not who, but someone decided that it would be a good idea to have some shooting practice using the Stirling sub-machine guns that remained in the armoury. So, armed with a dozen weapons, the boxes were carried down to the 30 yard range and all the hundreds of rounds were fired off in a couple of days shooting 'practice'.[27]

The last passing-out parade: Brigadier D.H. Nott inspects Kluang Platoon.
Brigadier Nott is followed by Lt E.A. Ireland, Major J.D. Reynolds and Sgt P. Spelman.
The recruit on the extreme right is Pte M.E. Hartiss.

7 THE DEPOT – IN RETROSPECT[1]

You obtain your first and memorable impression of the Regimental Depot on the first day you join the Army. While spending a tedious hour at Shrub Hill Station awaiting your transport, your mind is filled with anxious anticipation, and you build up an imaginary picture of what life is going to be like for the next few years.

After a somewhat shaky journey you arrive at the barracks where you are interrogated about personal history and background. After that you are issued with your kit which may or may not fit. On walking to the barrack room you may well see a frantic Sergeant tussling in the rain with his squad hoping to get some harmony into the drill. His voice and his language alone might make you wish, as I did, that you had never boarded that train to Worcester, but you are in the Army now!

A rigorous ten weeks training follows, and in this time everyone is supposed to acquire the basic rudiments of an infantryman's knowledge. Little things stick in one's memory: the day 'Arthur Rank' Gibbs pulled a film through by hand; the day water seeped into the alarm system and stood the whole barracks 'to'; days at Walton Hall [an infantry training base in Warwickshire], pleasant afternoons at Tyddesley Wood [rifle and light machine gun firing ranges near Pershore], the 'pantomime' on the assault course; the day either Elkin or Ingram blew 'cookhouse' for 'CO Orders' [the latter being the bugle calls blown to call those facing disciplinary action, whilst 'cookhouse' is blown when everyone is called to attend meals]; CSM Balchin's cherubic face, worthy of Raphael; 'Jet' Dovey's height, Corporals Till and Link on a motorbike on RSM's parade – all these kaleidoscopic impressions merge together when I think of Norton now. I think everyone enjoys his short stay at Norton, and perhaps some of the happiest army days are spent in training there, for it's certainly a good time – in retrospect!

As well as utilizing the training facilities available at Norton, recruits were able to take advantage of additional external training areas. One such was the Walton Hall Estate in Warwickshire, where field training, tactics, weapon training and lectures were carried out. In addition to the 30-metre ranges at the barracks, rifle and machine gun practice and grading was conducted at the larger shooting ranges at Tyddesley Wood near Pershore, a facility well known to all Worcestershire soldiers over many years.

Rifle and Light Machine Gun Ranges
under construction at Tyddesley Wood

8   Sport and Other Activities

Sports and leisure activities play an important part in supplementing military training and providing a welcome change in the soldiers' often repetitive routine. Sport provides exercise, assists in improving levels of fitness and promotes a competitive spirit. It instils and fosters a feeling of 'Esprit de Corps' and a sense of belonging that is imperative in any regiment.

The depot football team was always prominent in local leagues and much success was achieved in league and cup competitions. During the Second World War, 23 ITC were particularly successful, winning the Herefordshire County Cup in the 1944-45 season,

23 ITC Hereford County Cup Winners 1944-45
Standing, L to R: Ptes Goodall and Rollins, Cpl Cumberlidge, Pte Phillips, RSM Brown,
Ptes Swinnerton, Pearce, Thomas and Fowler
Sitting: L/Cpl Edwards, Lt-Col C.V.W. Court, MC, Sgt Ware, Capt. Bate, Cpl Reid

while in 1948 on the abolition of 29 PTC their football team fittingly went out in a blaze of glory, winning the prestigious Thursday Cup, beating the league champions RAF Defford 6-1 in the final.[1] The regiment produced a number of very fine players, perhaps the most outstanding of whom were Sergeant Alf Dalloway and RQMS 'Dinky' Shaw who played for their battalion and the regiment for many years; both also played for the full British Army side.

Sergeant A. 'Curly' Dalloway

Alf Dalloway joined the regiment in August 1919 and was to serve it in some capacity all of his working life. He was one of the most loved, respected and loyal men ever to serve in the regiment. He was posted to the 5th Battalion in Dublin and served with them from 1919 for three years. He then joined the 2nd Battalion in which he served for 16 years. After service in Germany, Plymouth and Malta he sailed to China and was stationed in Shanghai, Tiensin and Peking. While at Crownhill Barracks, Plymouth in 1930, Curly married his first wife Ivy and soon afterwards they were posted to Malta. There Ivy contracted tuberculosis and had to return to the UK with their 18-month-old daughter. In 1933 Curly was posted to China and the family were not reunited until he returned to Plymouth in 1936. During his time with the 2nd Battalion, Curly played football, hockey and cricket for the battalion. But it was at football that he excelled, playing for the regiment continuously for 16 years, ten of them as captain. He played for the British Army of the Rhine in 1927 and 1928 and for the full British Army side in 1929 and 1930. At the end of 1936 Curly, now a Sergeant, was posted to the depot. He served there in 1937 and 1938 before retiring after 18 years' service. On retirement he was employed as the Sergeants' Mess caterer, a job he did, except for a short break in 1939/40, until 1959 when the depot closed.

In January 1940 Curly and his family lost the majority of their possessions in a fire, during which their married quarters was severely damaged. Tragically, early in that year Ivy's health deteriorated and after a short spell in hospital she died in May 1940, leaving Curly to bring up his two young daughters. In 1943 Curly married his second wife May, a serving member of the ATS. They moved into the black and white thatched cottage close to the barracks in Norton village, which became known fondly as Dalloway's cottage, where his third daughter was born in 1944. He was to live there for 42 years.[2] In 1953 Curly was honoured to receive the Coronation Medal together with a citation, which he proudly hung on his cottage wall. When the depot closed to the regiment in 1959 Curly carried on manning the petrol pumps on the small parade ground opposite the Keep until 1962, when they were no longer required. Curly died at the age of 85 in 1986. His ashes were interred in Norton churchyard.

Cricket was a principal sport within the regiment and was played throughout the season against local sides on the cricket green. A major event in the Norton calendar was the annual cricket week which took place in the month of June. Matches played at the barracks and on the county ground were very popular and attracted good crowds.

One of the most accomplished players serving at the depot was Bandsman Jack Parkes, representing the regiment both as a serving soldier and civilian employee. A number of the depot players won representative honours, playing for the Worcestershire County side and for England. Leg spin bowler Roly Jenkins, a PT instructor at the barracks whose career started prior to the Second World War and went on until 1958, is fondly remembered for taking recruits out running while he accompanied them on his bike. Worcestershire opening batsman Peter Richardson, a National Serviceman[3] who played for Worcestershire from 1952 until 1958 before moving to Kent, also served as a PT instructor at the barracks: both won England caps. Richardson made 34 appearances for England, scoring 81 and 73 in his first test match and notably scored a century

Bandsman J. Parkes

Jack Parkes was one of those soldiers who spent their entire working life serving the regiment. Uniquely, Jack was born into the regiment for as soon as he was old enough, in 1916, he followed his father into the regiment, enlisting as a boy soldier. At the age of 16 he was too young to fight so spent what remained of the First World War at Norton Barracks. After the war he joined the 1st Battalion band and remained with them until he took his discharge in 1937. Jack Parkes was one of the finest all-round sportsmen the regiment ever had, and while serving in India repre-sented the 1st Battalion and All India at cricket, football and hockey for many years. When the battalion returned to England in 1931 he represented the regiment during many regimental cricket weeks, famously scoring an unbeaten century against the Worcestershire Gentlemen in June 1931. He was well educated but for some reason spurned promotion. As a first class musician he was happy playing his favourite instrument, the French horn, and remaining as Band Storeman.

On discharge he returned to Norton and lived with his mother, finding employ-ment at the depot, which allowed him to continue to play cricket and hockey. He was recalled for service in the Second World War, remaining at the depot with the band, under Bandmaster George Bixley. Demobbed for a second time in 1946, he again returned to work at the barracks, taking over the job as Barrack Storeman, a position he held until he retired in 1966. He was awarded the Imperial Service Medal in the same year. Jack's health deteriorated during 1967 and he died at Worcester's Ronkswood Hospital on 12 August 1968 at the age of 67. He was buried in St James' churchyard, Norton, his funeral attended by many members of the regiment.

Worcestershire Regiment cricket team 1928
Standing, L to R: Capt. P.W. Hargreaves, Bandsman J. Parkes, CSM Denton,
Capt. G.A. Sheppard, Lt F.W. Allen, CSM Harling, Mr G.C. Cooper,
CQMS Singleton (umpire)
Sitting: Maj. G.St.L. Davies, Lt-Col A.C. Johnston, Lt-Col H.A. Fulton, Maj. R.E. Vyvyan

Worcestershire Regiment cricket team 1962
Standing, L to R: Scorer, Lt-Col A.F.J.G. Jackson, Cpl A. Mackie, 2/Lt R. Palmer,
Capt. G.E. Gibbons, Capt. J.T. Wilson, Capt. A.M. Martyn, Mr A. Dalloway (umpire)
Seated: Maj. T.A. Batchelar, Capt. E.B. Wilson, Maj. A.M. Gabb,
Lt-Col P.G.B. Hall, Capt. G.F. Owens

against Australia in a test match at Old Trafford in 1956, during which the legendary England spinner Jim Laker took 19 Australian wickets.

Boxing, particularly recruit boxing tournaments, rugby, field hockey, athletics and cross country running were all popular sports and, as befits an infantry training depot, competition shooting played a major part in depot pursuits. The depot shooting teams

Depot shooting team 1955
Back Row, L to R: Ptes F. Sharp, K. Rouse, J. James, J. Dutton, P. Russell, R. Morgan,
Drummer J. Green
Centre Row: L/Cpl J. Groves, Cpls M. Layland, B. Hinsley, J. Duffield, B. Griffiths,
L/Cpl P. Wood
Front Row: Sgt J. Pountney, Sgt T. Bell, Lt P.G. Dunn, Maj. J.D. Ricketts, DSO,
Lt D.J. Bezzant, C/Sgt R. Astbury, Sgt K. Newstead

Croome Hunt at Norton Barracks, c.1936

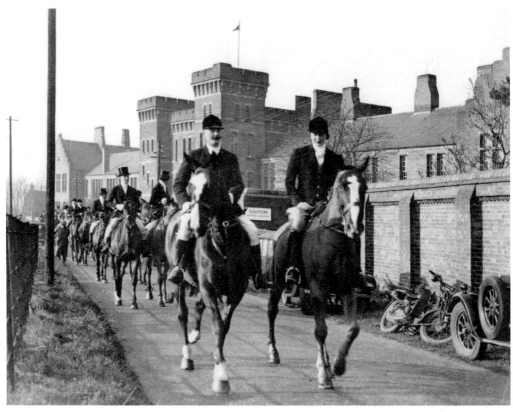

Lord Coventry and Lady Lygon leading out the Croome Hunt, c.1937

enjoyed sustained success over many years in both Army Command shooting competitions and the prestigious annual events at Bisley.

Officers of the depot had ridden with the Croome Hunt from the very early days, indeed from the opening of Norton Barracks. Many hours were spent traversing the countryside around Norton with riders often hacking back to barracks across country with darkness approaching.[4] On arrival at the depot, Lieutenant C.P. Vaughan was asked two questions by his CO, Major E.L.G. Lawrence. The first was 'Do you ride?' The second 'Do you have a horse?' In fact Peter Vaughan was much more interested in motor racing, but he turned out to hunt once a week.[5] The highlight of the hunting season was the annual Boxing Day Meet, with the hunt and its followers assembling at the barracks. Mrs Dorothy Ricketts remembered that, 'On Boxing Day the depot welcomed the Croome Hunt with stirrup cups of Mr Oldham's renowned rum punch.'[6]

For many years the barracks was host to one of the most important of regimental occasions, the annual reunion. The first reunion took place on Saturday 31 October 1925 (Gheluvelt Day), in the Shire Hall in Worcester. Later it moved to Norton Barracks and was held on a Saturday in June, in the same week as Cricket Week and the officers' cocktail party. It was held at the barracks until 1976 then at various loca-

The Four Colonels of the Regiment at the Regimental Reunion 29 June 1968
L to R: Brigadier B.C.S. Clarke, DSO; General Sir Richard Gale, GCB, KBE, DSO, MC;
Brigadier D.H. Nott, DSO, OBE, MC, DL; Colonel T.J. Bowen, MC

tions including the racecourse on Pitchcroft, in Kidderminster, and at Sixways, the Worcester Warriors Rugby ground. The reunion, always well attended, is still looked upon by many ex-members of the regiment as a memorable occasion, and the chance to meet old comrades and renew old friendships is eagerly anticipated.

Leisure time for off duty soldiers was often spent in the City of Worcester where all of the usual facilities – the cinema, dancing, the local pubs and restaurants – were available. Many will remember the blue buses operated between the city and the barracks by 'Old Man Marko' (Mr Marks) and his daughter Sylvia. From the late 1940s up to the mid 1950s Sylvia used to drive the buses and would permit no swearing or bad behaviour. Any offender would be put off the bus and made to find his own way home. The last bus to the barracks was always at 11pm.[7]

Old Man Marko's blue bus. Sylvia Marks is standing centre front.

9 REGIMENTAL HEADQUARTERS

On the closure of the depot, a Regimental Headquarters (RHQ) was formed at the barracks in the old Officers' Mess. Its small establishment consisted of two Retired Officers, a Clerical Officer, a storeman and a typist. Lt-Col C.P. Vaughan was appointed RO II and assumed command of RHQ, which was given a charter that defined its responsibilities as follows:

1. Secretariat to the Colonel of the Regiment
2. Agent of the Regiment for its recruiting
3. Handling of Regimental and Trustee funds
4. Secretariat to the Regimental Committee and liaison with the Worcestershire Regimental Association
5. Care of Regimental silver and property
6. Regimental clubs, functions and reunions
7. Regimental Journal
8. Care and Maintenance of Museum and Historical Records
9. Liaison with County Civic Authorities, TA and Cadets
10. Representing the Colonel of the Regiment at functions.

Early in 1960 a bronze plaque was placed on the entrance to the Keep to commemorate the service of soldiers of the Worcestershire Regiment who over the many years had passed through Norton Barracks.

The late 1950s and early 1960s saw the site occupied by a number of battalions who moved into the barracks

The First (Bronze) Memorial Plaque

Field Marshal B.L. Montgomery with Major J.D. Reynolds at Norton Barracks, March 1959

for varying periods of time. The 1ˢᵗ Battalion, the Sherwood Foresters were briefly in residence from January to June 1958, followed by the Royal Irish Fusiliers. The 1ˢᵗ Battalion, the Warwickshire Regiment were in residence when in March 1959 they were inspected by Field Marshal B.L. Montgomery, 1st Viscount Montgomery of Alamein, during a farewell parade prior to their posting to Aden.

The 1ˢᵗ Battalion the Royal Inniskilling Fusiliers were temporarily in residence between December 1959 and January 1960 prior to sailing for Kenya. In 1960 the 1ˢᵗ Battalion Worcestershire Regiment returned home from the West Indies, where they were welcomed home by the city with a ceremonial parade on 21 May. The salute was taken by the Colonel of the Regiment, General Sir Richard Gale who, with the Mayor of Worcester inspected the battalion on parade. On 16 July General Gale presented new Colours to the battalion on the green.

While at the barracks, as well as being preoccupied with recruiting, the battalion was twice deployed. The first was to participate in a training exercise in Libya in 1961. The second was go to British Honduras when, after the country had been struck by Hurricane Hattie, the battalion was called upon to provide aid and assistance to the inhabitants.

During their time at the barracks the opportunity to escape before the end of the working week was too much for some who lived locally; so on Friday afternoons, much to the annoyance of the staff, there was often an exodus from the barracks before the bugler blew for the official end of the working day, despite the fact that the regimental police patrolled the road to Worcester. The battalion eventually left Norton Barracks for Germany in 1962.

The 1ˢᵗ Battalion, South Wales Borderers took up residence from November 1962 to November 1963, followed by the 1ˢᵗ Battalion, Lancashire Fusiliers who occupied the Barracks in 1964-65. The Royal Inniskilling Fusiliers returned and were in residence from 1967 to 1968. Following an amalgamation parade on the 1 July 1968, they became the 1ˢᵗ Battalion, Royal Irish Rangers and served at Norton until leaving in November 1968.

General Sir R.N. Gale, GCB, KBE, DSO, MC, presents the Queens Colour to the 1ˢᵗ Battalion on the drill square, July 1960

1ˢᵗ Battalion Worcestershire Regiment Officers, 1962
Back Row, L to R: Lt D.W. Reeve, 2/Lt R.J. Waters, Lt G.E. Gibbons, Capt. A.M. Martyn,
Capt. A.W.S. Hargrave, Capt. A.N. Nisbet, Capt. E.A. Ireland, Capt. H.J. Lowles,
Lt A.L.O. Jerram, Lt P.K. Holmes, 2/Lt N. Channing Williams, 2/Lt J.J. Hall.
Front Row: Capt. R.A.U. Richards, Maj. J.H.C. Crompton, Maj. M.R. Ellis, Lt-Col P.G.B.
Hall, Maj. R.G.A. Leman, Maj. H.W. Sargeant, Maj. H. Knox, Maj. A.M. Gabb

Early in 1969, 14th Signal Regiment (Royal Signals) moved into Norton Barracks, having moved from Robin Hood Barracks in Gloucester, and were destined to stay for a considerable period. During their time in Worcester they formed a close relationship with the regiment and the local community. Their move had been intended to be a permanent one, but on their amalgamation with 30th Signal Regiment at Blandford, the regiment eventually moved out, their rear party leaving in January 1977. During their time at Norton, nearly eight years, the regiment endeared themselves to and formed a close association with RHQ and fostered close links with the city and county, taking a full part in Remembrance Day parades and acting as hosts to Soldiers, Sailors and Airmen's Families Association receptions, as well as supporting many functions in aid of the Army Benevolent Fund.[1] Indeed, all temporary resident units provided valuable assistance to the small RHQ staff, particularly in hosting key events such as the annual reunion. On leaving Norton the 14th Signal Regiment Adjutant, Capt. Richard Holmes, wrote:

> 14th Signal Regiment is very sorry to be leaving Worcester. We shall miss the sturdy homeliness of Norton Barracks; the trees round the green, the view of the cathedral tower across the square. We are especially sad that our departure may mean the final closure of the barracks, but we are proud to have followed those thousands of soldiers of the Worcestershire Regiment who have marched through the gates to serve their country in peace and war.[2]

Before the last members of the 14th Signal Regiment left Norton in January 1977 the Ministry of Defence announced its intention to close the barracks two months later. At this stage no decision had been made on the future location of the Regimental HQ, but it was decided to hold one last regimental cocktail party in the old depot mess. This was held on 28 February and the Regimental Mess members responded magnificently with over 180 serving and retired officers and their guests attending. The Colonel of the Regiment, Colonel T.J. Bowen presided and his successor, Brigadier P.G.L. Litton attended, together with two previous Colonels of the Regiment, General Sir R.N. Gale and Brigadier D.H. Nott. The RHQ remained in the depot Mess until June 1978 when it moved to Building 97, a brick building on the extremity of the western side of the new camp. This building had previously been used as the ATS Mess during the Second World War and as the headquarters of 159 Infantry Brigade (TA). After the war it was used by the 14th Signal Regiment as a secure cypher building.

In 1980 the bronze commemorative plaque was surreptitiously removed from its place on the Keep. Later, having been missing for two and a half years, it was found in 1983 in the possession of a Yeomanry Regiment. Who had taken it was never revealed, but it was returned to the regiment after letters had been exchanged between the two units. At the suggestion of the Worcester Branch of the Regimental Association a new slate plaque was procured to be placed high on the wall (to discourage vandals) at the front of the Keep. On Sunday 4 June 1995 the new plaque replacing the original bronze

plaque, now in the Regimental Museum, was unveiled. The ceremony was attended by over a hundred former members of the regiment, families, friends and civic dignitaries led by the Mayor of Worcester. The Reverend Ian Reid, Vicar of St James the Great in Norton, dedicated the plaque to those who had served the regiment and their country. Colonel John Reynolds, the last officer to command the Regimental Depot, unveiled the plaque, reminding all that Norton Barracks would always be the symbolic home of the Worcestershire Regiment.[3] The plaque can still be seen, located high up on the wall of the old Keep.

People passing Building 97 – which had heavy bars on the windows, and for some time had a tall aerial and was surrounded by a chainlink fence – must have wondered what sinister activities went on there. On retiring after working there for three years Mrs Gillian Jones wrote:

Colonel J.D. Reynolds unveiling the new Memorial Plaque, June 1995

There is the regimental magazine to produce and the results are seen twice each year, but the office also generates a wide variety of additional work. It prepares the greetings to be despatched when the Battle Honours of the Regiment are remembered, the reports to be written following interviews of young men aspiring to join as an officer, and countless replies to enquiries as to what grandad or uncle did in the war. These are always prepared with care and include whatever snippets of interest can be found. There are persuasive letters encouraging donations for the Regimental Museum, letters of condolence on the death of former comrades and replies to members of the regiment in need of a grant because of hardship. The personal touch of the HQ pleases me as an outsider – notification of an illness or hospitalisation is conveyed to those who may wish to visit and congratulatory notes are sent to those about to marry. Items for the shop need to be ordered, reports of planning are drafted and finalised. The work is exceptionally varied.[4]

On 1 September 2007 after a further reorganisation of the British Army, the Worcestershire and Sherwood Foresters Regiment was incorporated into the Mercian Regiment as the 2nd Battalion, joining the Staffordshire Regiment and the Cheshire

Regiment in the new formation. The Regimental Headquarters in Building 97 became an outstation of RHQ, the Mercian Regiment. Consequently the work of RHQ was rationalised and many of Norton's responsibilities were taken over by RHQ staff at Lichfield. The RHQ at Norton under the Regimental Secretary, Major R.S. Prophet retained responsibility for officer recruitment, the Regimental Journal, liaison with local dignitaries and the Regimental Museum.

The last link between the regiment and the barracks site was broken after almost 134 years with the final closure of the RHQ and the removal of the Regimental Archives to the TA Centre in Worcester. On Sunday 20 March 2011 veterans and their families assembled at RHQ to witness what was an emotional ceremony to mark the closure. The Regimental and British Legion Standards were lowered, the Last Post sounded and Reveille rang out before 90 members of the Regimental Association and other veterans marched past. The Parade Commander was Colonel John Reynolds, the last five regimental secretaries brought up the rear, while order was maintained by Sergeant Major Bryn Knowles. Also in attendance were the Mercian Regimental Mascot, Derby the Swaledale ram, and his two handlers. The salute was taken by the Mayor of Worcester, Mike Layland, himself a former regimental physical training instructor at the barracks, accompanied by Linda Robinson, chairman of Wychavon District Council. Afterwards refreshments were served to the crowd of about 200 people who had attended the parade by the ladies of the Worcester Branch of the Regimental Association.

No account of the Regimental HQ would be complete without acknowledging the valued contribution of those civilians who worked there and provided continuity as Regimental Secretaries came and went.

Having served at Norton with the ATS, Mrs Turner stayed on for some time in the Officers' Mess. Miss Bennett, who had also served in the ATS, was a knowledgeable figure in the office. She had cycled up the long hill on the Bath Road each day for many years and her first act on retirement was to dump her bicycle on the local tip to signal her delight at not having to do so again. Mrs Pittaway gave sterling service in both the Officers' Mess and the Museum. Mrs Griffiths and Mrs Jenny Shenton did valuable work on the typewriter then the computer while trying to decipher the handwriting of successive regimental secretaries. Mrs Angela Arthur deserves a special mention for managing the office so efficiently while guiding the last five regimental secretaries as they came and went, and for establishing cordial relations with all who visited RHQ.

10   THE DEPOT AND NORTON PARISH CHURCH

The regimental depot, being located within the parish boundary, has enjoyed very close ties with the village of Norton Juxta Kempsey and with its church, St James the Great, ever since the occupation of the barracks in 1877. Unusually, no church was built within the barracks as it had previously been decided that the soldiers should use the village church. Following the building of the barracks, Norton became a garrison village and St James the Great, a garrison church.[1] As a direct result of that decision, made during the construction of the barracks, which coincided with extensive restoration work at the church, a new south aisle was added to the church in 1875. On Sundays depot staff and the recruits would muster for church parade and march to Norton Church for the morning service, often accompanied by the Regimental Band. The vicar of St James was also appointed the official padre to the barracks.

Church of St James the Great at Norton Juxta Kempsey

The churchyard at St James' contains the graves of several old Worcestershire Regiment men who died while serving at the depot or who settled in the area on completion of their service and lived out the rest of their lives close by, some of them in the village itself. Inside the church there is a brass tablet to the memory of Captain A.G.M. Graham, who died at Le Touret on 22 December 1914. Another commemorates Lt-Col C.F. Wodehouse, DSO, killed in action at Neuve Chappelle on 12 March 1915. More recently, the remains of Brigadier D.H. Nott, Sgt 'Curly' Dalloway and his wife May, Sgt Frank Lester, C/Sgt John Sopp, Bandsman Jack Parkes and others have been laid to rest in Norton churchyard. Because of the close connection between the regiment and the church, Battalion Colours were laid up in the south aisle: the 2nd Battalion Colours 1907-30 were laid up on 14 September 1930 and the 3rd (Militia) Battalion Colours 1886-1922 on 21 July 1933. On the south wall a memorial to men of the regiment was unveiled on 28 October 1949 by Brigadier B.C.S. Clarke, the Colonel of the Worcestershire Regiment. It reads:

In memory of all ranks of the Regiment sometime members of the congregation of
Norton Church who gave their lives in the wars
1914-18 and 1939-45

Two of the Worcestershire Regiment graves in Norton churchyard

11   THE REGIMENTAL MUSEUM

The Regimental Museum, originally established by depot staff at Norton Barracks in 1923,[1] spent its first 37 years in various locations within the barracks and the adjoining Second World War hutted camp. Initially located in the Officers' Mess, Major H.FitzM. Stacke worked determinedly to establish and then improve the museum. It was moved to the Keep in 1935, and was housed in temporary hutments during the Second World

A view of the museum exhibits in the Officers' Mess ante-room

War. After the war it was taken back into the depot and housed in accommodation on the top floor of Farrington Block. Further development was undertaken by Major H.P.E. Pereira, who was responsible for its subsequent expansion and layout. It was he who managed its affairs from 1944 to 1948.[2] By the time he left the Army in 1948, Pat Pereira had established what was at the time one of the finest regimental museums in Britain. He left to become curator of the United Services Museum in Edinburgh Castle, a post he held until his untimely death at the age of 49 in 1955. No reference to the museum would be complete without mentioning the care lavished upon it by Mr Frank Lester. Frank took charge of the day to day running of the museum in 1935; it remained under his unfailing guardianship until his death in 1950. Mr George Chapman, who had also served in the regiment during the First World War, and whose son was killed in France in 1940 while serving in the 7th Battalion, succeeded Mr Lester as custodian of the museum. Both his and his son's medals are in the museum collection. In later years as the volume of work increased, the regiment was fortunate enough to have two valued volunteers, Lt-Col C.P. Love, TD, who answered enquiries from the public and Group Captain John Barker, who catalogued the medal collection.

The permanent display of the Worcestershire Regiment Museum was moved from Norton Barracks to Worcester City Museum and Art Gallery, in Foregate Street, Worcester in 1970.

Sergeant F. Lester

The personification of a 'faithful' Worcestershire soldier, Frank Lester, joined the regiment in 1892. After completing his recruit training at Norton Barracks he joined the 2nd Battalion at the Curragh in Ireland. He served in Aldershot and then joined the 1st Battalion in India. He returned to the UK in 1899, serving in the Crownhill Barracks in Plymouth and at Aldershot to prepare for the South African War. After service in England and South Africa, he again went to war and served on the Western Front in France during the First World War. He served throughout from Mons in 1914 until he was wounded in November 1918, sustaining an injury which resulted in his losing one of his legs. After discharge he moved into one of the regimental cottages outside the barracks and was employed within the depot. As custodian of the regimental museum and therefore of so much history and tradition, he was known to many of the soldiers who passed through the barracks. He was one of a select number of men who served the regiment first as a soldier and then as a civilian. Frank died after a long illness in April 1950 at the age of 76 and was buried with full military honours in Norton churchyard.[3] His funeral was attended by the Colonel of the Regiment, Brigadier B.C.S. Clarke, DSO, Lt-Col Sir John and Lady Reddie and numerous other officers, NCOs and other ranks, along with past members of the regiment. (Sir John Reddie had been knighted for services to soldiers' welfare.)[4]

A view of the museum exhibits in Farrington Block, c.1968

Part of the museum display in 2015

By the early 1990s it was realised that it needed to be updated and refreshed in order to appeal to a public with little knowledge or experience of the Army. In 1994, a project team was formed with the task of planning the refurbishment, and they asked the National Army Museum to produce a design proposal for a new display. In 1996, the fundraising started, and by October 2002 most of the funding had been secured. The museum was closed and work started in earnest. The city council carried out the building work required on the galleries while conservation work was carried out on the objects and the detailed layout of new galleries was planned in conjunction with the National Army Museum, who provided the design input and supervised the contractors. The refurbished galleries, which were opened to the public on 28 July 2003, now include the Worcestershire Regiment and Yeomanry collections (previously in separate galleries) plus part of the city council's Worcester at War collection.

12   AFTERMATH – THE BARRACKS SITE NOW

Norton Barracks, the home of the Worcestershire Regiment, was sold to property developers in 1982. After changing hands several times it was left to deteriorate for some years before, in 1993, the bulldozers moved in to demolish most of the historic buildings. The Keep block was spared because, before the barracks was sold, the regimental secretary, Colonel J.D. Ricketts, had arranged for it to be Grade 2 listed, much to the annoyance of the Ministry of Defence because the listing complicated its sale. Sam Beard, ever to the forefront in his efforts to secure retention of the Keep and other buildings and constantly watchful over his beloved barracks, expressed his feelings as follows:

> The sad old Barracks broods
> O'er desolate Keep and square
> Gone all the pride and honour
> The 'Worcesters' once had there
>
> Gone too so many heroes
> Who neath their famous star
> Held high England's honour
> In battles near and far
>
> Above the Barrack doorways
> The faded names remain
> Of Charlemont and Farrington
> Fount of the 'Worcesters' fame
>
> Old Soldiers to your memory
> This ruined Barracks stands –
> No sentry at the Keep gate
> No rousing marching bands

No bugler to sound 'Retreat'
No sergeants on the square
Sad monument to your sacrifice
All peace and quiet there

The main site has now been developed as residential properties; new homes occupy the space where once soldiers marched. Of the old buildings few remain: the accommodation blocks Farrington and Charlemont, Higginson and Jacob, the old parade ground, the 19th-century other ranks married quarters and the hospital are among the many demolished.

The Keep has been converted into apartments. The Green remains and still hosts cricket matches. The old Sergeants' Mess, still recognisable, is now the Clubhouse of Worcester Norton Sports Club and the firing ranges continue to function as such under the aegis of Worcester Norton Shooting Club.

Several ex-members of the regiment have bought homes on the site and returned to live on that 'hallowed ground'. Jack Bastable arrived at Norton Barracks from the Junior Leaders Regiment in the mid '50s. After serving his time, including duty at the depot, in Germany, Belize and Jamaica, he was discharged to Civvie Street in the 1960s wondering if he had done the right thing in leaving the Army. Then in 1997:

The derelict Keep prior to redevelopment

I am back now. I have just paid £70,000 for the privilege of buying a house on the same site. Can you believe that? It is a new housing estate. I drink in the local pub, which used to be the Sgts' Mess. When leaving the pub, with some of the residents, I walk across the cricket pitch, past the Keep – which is now apartments – then onto the road where the main drill square used to be (I am still scared to put my hands in my pockets). I tell people I am with that they are walking on sacred ground. I get a few strange glances but you know what I mean.[1]

The old cricket green and Sergeants' Mess, now Worcester Norton Sports Club

Aerial view of Norton Barracks post development (c.2002).
The Keep, with its attached wings, is centre right below the cricket green which, with the old Sergeants' Mess and the firing ranges are all that remain. The surrounding streets and buildings, many bearing names associated with the regiment, lie on ground previously occupied by buildings that once formed part of Norton Barracks.

The Norton Barracks known to thousands of soldiers of the Worcestershire Regiment and to recruits of many other regiments is no more. What remains of the original buildings will forever act as a reminder of the events that have taken place there since it was first occupied. Many old soldiers will identify with the feelings expressed by Mrs Dorothy Ricketts when, in 2006, she wrote:

> Today the part of the barracks which faces the road looks the same thanks to a preservation order, but the Officers' Mess, Keren House, the Keep, the former offices and the NAAFI have all been converted into flats. Charlemont and Farrington and many other buildings have been demolished, but the Green and the chestnut trees are still there. In my imagination I can still hear bugles, marching feet and brisk orders. Then as now Norton Barracks has its place in regimental history and, for a short time, I was privileged to share in its memories of people and events.[2]

Perhaps the words of Colonel John Reynolds are the most appropriate with which to end this short history:

> In 1957 I became Depot Commander, and saw out the last 18 months of the depot. Those were happy days, living in Keren House, putting up General Gale when he came to inspect us (I remember catching him one afternoon on his knees in the drawing-room, playing hide-and-seek with my young daughter!) Yes I have many memories of Norton Barracks. What a shame it is no longer. Though one must be thankful that the Keep is still the same shape, if seen at a distance. I often wonder what it is like having your sitting room in the old Keep archway – and presumably your kitchen, etc, in the old cells! There must be lots of ghosts around.[3]

APPENDIX I   THE REGIMENTAL SIGNIFICANCE OF THE STREET NAMES ON THE FORMER MILITARY SITE

Battle honours are awarded to regiments for displaying exceptional devotion to duty and playing a major part in battles and campaigns. The Worcestershire Regiment and its predecessors, the 29th and 36th regiments, were awarded 22 honours between 1706 and 1902, of which 11 were awarded for the Peninsular campaign of 1808-1814, 80 for the First World War 1914-18, and 36 for the Second World War 1939-45. All except two of the street names listed below commemorate some of these.

Cambrai Drive. There were two major battles near the French town of Cambrai in 1917 in which six battalions of the regiment took part. Cambrai is noted for the first use of tanks in significant numbers. During the battle they successfully supported the infantry assault and severely affected the morale of the defending German army.

Corunna Close. In 1809 the 36th Regiment retreated over 250 miles of mountainous country in Spain and stood to fight at Corunna. After having to repel repeated attacks, the French were defeated and most of the British troops were able to embark safely for England, though their commander Lieutenant-General Sir John Moore was killed.

Dunkirk Drive. The 7th and 8th Battalions of the regiment took part in the retreat to Dunkirk in France in 1940. In the face of sustained German pressure during which many were killed or captured, many members of the British Expeditionary Force along with thousands of other allied soldiers were famously evacuated from the port and surrounding beaches by an armada of small ships.

Gallipoli Drive. From the spring of 1915 until January 1916 the 4th and 9th Battalions of the regiment fought in the bitter nine-month campaign against entrenched Turkish forces on the Gallipoli Peninsula in the Dardanelles, before finally being evacuated to Egypt.

Gazala Drive. The 1st Battalion occupied and held a defensive position along the coast road in a bid to hold up the enemy during the battle of Gazala in North Africa in May and June 1942. Against Field Marshal Rommel's famed German Afrika Corps they fought a spirited action before withdrawing into Tobruk.

The Wire Cutters. Men of the Worcestershire Regiment at work at Gallipoli, from a drawing by Gilbert Holliday. (Regimental Museum)

Keren Drive. After two previous battles had resulted in stalemate, the 1ˢᵗ Battalion was part of the 29ᵗʰ Indian Brigade which captured a strongly held Italian position in the mountains of Eritrea after bitter fighting during the Third Battle of Keren in March 1941.

Kohima Drive. The 7ᵗʰ Battalion was heavily involved in the successful defence of the Indian town of Kohima against strong Japanese forces at the start of the Burma campaign in 1944. Noted as the turning point of the Japanese offensive into India, the battle led to the abandonment of the Imphal Ridge by the Japanese and the relief of Imphal. The National Army Museum voted this as Britain's greatest battle.

Mandalay Drive. During the British drive into Burma in March 1945, the retreating Japanese army were strongly entrenched in defensive positions in and around the Burmese city of Mandalay. The 2ⁿᵈ Battalion of the regiment was instrumental in expelling the Japanese from and liberating the city, and along with the 7ᵗʰ Battalion played a major role in the both the defence of India and in the campaign in Burma.

Mons Drive. The 2ⁿᵈ and 3ʳᵈ Battalions, having landed in France and advanced into Belgium as part of the British Expeditionary Force in August 1914, took part in the fighting retreat from Mons in the face of the German advance in August and September 1914.

Nive Gardens. After the battle of Nivelle in late 1813, towards the end of the Peninsular War, the French General Soult had formed his defences around the town of Bayonne. The 36ᵗʰ crossed the River Nive in southern France from west to east to attack the French army defending the town. Amid fierce fighting they were forced to re-cross the river to frustrate an attack threatening their left flank, a daunting manoeuvre at that time.

Nivelle Grove. After the British had taken the town of San Sebastian, the 36th helped to secure Wellington's right flank by capturing a key fortification in southern France during the battle of Nivelle in November 1813. This led to the defeat of the French and the retreat of their army.

Peninsula Road. This honour was awarded to both the 29th and 36th in recognition of their contribution during the Peninsular War fought in Portugal, Spain and France from 1808 to 1814.

Ramillies Drive. This was the regiment's first battle honour. Farrington's Regiment, later the 29th, was part of the Duke of Marlborough's army which took part in the attack on Ramillies during this battle in the War of the Spanish Succession in Flanders in 1706. It was later said to be the battle which decided the fate of the Netherlands.

Regiment Close. Most of the houses in this street were built for married men on the staff of the depot.

Rolica Fields. The 29th and 36th were involved in this, the first battle of the Peninsular War in Portugal in 1808, a battle in which both regiments were destined to play a major part. The 29th Regiment led the attack on the heights of Columbeira on 17 July during which Lt-Col George Lake, their commanding officer, was amongst those killed. With additional forces brought up in support, this action was instrumental in defeating the French.

Lt-Col George Lake

St Helena Court. Not a regimental battle, but the willow tree in one corner is alleged to be a cutting taken from the tree near Napoleon's grave in St Helena.

Salamanca Drive. The 36th fought at the battle of Salamanca during the Peninsular War under Wellington in 1812. Arriving on 17 June 1812 they immediately commenced operations against the forts at Salamanca. Meeting fierce French resistance the battle lasted until 22 July when the enemy finally fled.

Seine Close. In August 1944, following the allied advance from Normandy, Operation Neptune, the crossing of the River Seine began. In XXX Corps the 43rd Division was given the task of crossing at Vernon. As part of that formation the 1st Battalion was the first complete unit to cross the river against stiff German opposition and secured their objective by reaching Vernonnet. By 28 August they had consolidated their position and were able to resupply and attend to the wounded.

Sobraon Crescent. The 29th fought in this battle against the entrenched Sikhs during the conquest of the Punjab in India in 1846. The 29th, supported by two native battalions, dashed towards the ramparts which the Sihks had erected. After two unsuccessful charges, the 29th succeeded in reaching the first Sikh trenches. The enemy suffered terrible carnage and by the end of the battle had lost some 10,000 men and 67 guns. The British losses were also heavy, suffering 2,383 killed or wounded, among which the 29th's casualties numbered 186 out of a total strength of 552.

Somme Crescent. Ten battalions of the regiment were involved in the many battles fought along the River Somme in France during 1916 and 1918. The battles of the Somme saw some of the fiercest fighting of the war with the British suffering some 60,000 men killed or wounded on the first day, 1 July 1916.

Talavera Road. The 29th under Wellington captured a strategically important hill in Spain from the French in this battle in the Peninsular War in 1809. During the battle both sides lost about a quarter of their men, causing Wellington to say 'Talavera was the hardest fought battle of modern times.'

Toulouse Drive. The 36th were participants in the battle of Toulouse, the final battle of the Peninsular War and fought on French soil. After fierce fighting in which the British and French suffered combined casualties of nearly 8,000 men, General Soult, the French commander, signed an armistice thus ending the war on 17 April 1814. Toulouse proved to have been a tragic waste of life and a battle that need never have been fought as, after the battle, news was received that Napoleon had abdicated four days earlier.

Vimiera Close. This was the second battle in the Peninsular War in 1808 following which Sir Arthur Wellesley, later Lord Wellington, wrote of the 36th: 'The regular and orderly conduct of this corps throughout the service, and the gallantry and discipline in action have been conspicuous. The 36th is an example to the army.'

Ypres Close. Ten battalions of the regiment were involved in the numerous battles around the Belgian City of Ypres. Forming a salient surrounded on three sides and heavily shelled by German forces throughout, Ypres did not fall during the First World War. The regiment was involved in battles around Ypres in 1914, 1915, the notorious third Battle of Ypres (Passchendaele) in 1917, and again in 1918.

APPENDIX II COMMANDING OFFICERS & REGIMENTAL SECRETARIES

29 Regimental District Brigade Commanders

1877   Colonel Fitz Wm. F. Hunter ++

1882   Colonel R.E. Carr

1887   Colonel F.C. Ruxton

1892   Colonel C.P. Temple, DSO

1895   Colonel H.J. de B de Berniere

1902   Brevet Colonel W.S. Clarke

1905   Regimental District Brigade closed and Norton Barracks became a Regimental Depot

22 Regimental Depot and Worcestershire Regimental Depot Commanders

1881   Brevet Lieutenant Colonel St John Willans

1882   Brevet Lieutenant Colonel R.B. Lloyd

1885   Major J.L. Rose

1887   Major W.J. Browne

1889   Major G.W.F. Claremont

1891   Major E.H.St.L. Clarke

1894   Major O.H. Oakes

1897   Major A.W. Lennox-Conynham

1899   Major J. Chichester

1900   Major W.H. Thackwell

1902   Major G.N. Monro

1904   Major E. Bell

1907   Major C.B. Westmacott

1908   Major C.H. Bennett, DSO

1911   Major J.M. Reddie

1913   Major C.H. Palmer

1914   Brevet Colonel C.M. Edwards

1916   Lieutenant Colonel C.E. Greenway

1917   Lieutenant Colonel W.R. Chichester

1919	Major E.T.J. Kerans, DSO
1920	Major H.St.J. Jefferies
1922	Brevet Lieutenant Colonel J.O. Nelson, OBE
1923	Major B.C.S. Clarke, DSO
1926	Major J.F. Leman, DSO
1929	Major J.H. Pelly
1932	Major C. Deakin, OBE
1935	Major E.L.G. Lawrence, DSO, MC
1937	Major R.H.M. Lee
1939	Lieutenant Colonel J.F. Leman, DSO*
1939	Lieutenant Colonel R.H.M Lee, OBE*
1941	Lieutenant Colonel S.A. Gabb, OBE, MC*
1944	Lieutenant Colonel F.G. Rogers*
1945	Lieutenant Colonel L.G.H. Bryant*
1948	Major J.H.A. Dean
1951	Major J.B. Brierley, MBE, MC
1953	Major A.H. Nott
1955	Major J.D. Ricketts, DSO
1957	Major J.D. Reynolds, MC
1959	Closure of Depot at Norton Barracks

++ First Regimental Brigade Depot and Regimental District Brigade Commander
* Infantry Training Centre Commanders

Regimental Secretaries 1959-2011

1970	Lt-Col C.P. Vaughan, DSO, DL; Assistant, Lt-Col J.D. Ricketts, DSO, JP
1975	Lt-Col J.D. Ricketts, DSO, JP; Assistant, Col J.W.B. Stuart, MBE, MC
	(1977) Lt-Col K.G. Allen
1980	Lt-Col K.G. Allen, DL; Assistant, Maj. J.M. Brazier
	(1986) Lt-Col A.M. Gabb, OBE
1987	Lt-Col A.M. Gabb, OBE; Assistant, Lt-Col C.E. Potts, OBE
1990	Lt-Col C.E. Potts, OBE; Assistant, Lt-Col A.M. Gabb, OBE
	(1991) Maj. A.S. Noble
1993	Col H.J. Lowles, CBE; Assistant, Maj. A.S. Noble
	(1995) Maj. D.W. Reeve
2000	Maj. D.W. Reeve, MBE; Assistant, Maj. R.S. Prophet
2002	Maj. R.S. Prophet; Assistant, Maj. M.J. Green

GLOSSARY OF ABBREVIATIONS

Miscellaneous

ATS	Auxiliary Territorial Service
BEF	British Expeditionary Force
Brevet rank	A commission appointing an officer to a higher rank without increase in pay and with limited powers of that rank. Often awarded for gallantry or meritorious conduct
CO	Commanding Officer
HRH	His/Her Royal Highness
MA	Master of Arts
MT	Motor Transport
NAAFI	Navy Army and Air Force Institute
NCO	Non Commissioned Officer
OC	Officer Commanding
OCTU	Officer Cadet Training Unit
OTC	Officer Training Corps
PMC	President of the Mess Committee
PT	Physical Training
PTC	Primary Training Centre
POW	Prisoner of War
RA	Royal Artillery
RE	Royal Engineers
RHQ	Regimental Headquarters
RO	Retired Officer
SSAFA	Soldiers Sailors and Airmen's Families Association
TA	Territorial Army
USAF	United States Air Force

Honours, Decorations and Awards

CB	Companion of The Most Honourable Order of the Bath
CBE	Commander of The Most Excellent Order of the British Empire
CMG	Companion of The Most Distinguished Order of Saint Michael and Saint George
DL	Deputy Lieutenant
DSO	Distinguished Service Order
GCB	Knight Grand Cross of The Most Honourable Order of the Bath
KBE	Knight Commander of The Most Excellent Order of the British Empire
KCMG	Knight Commander of the Order of St Michael and St George
KCSI	Knight Commander of the Star of India
MBE	Member of The Most Excellent Order of the British Empire
MC	Military Cross
MM	Military Medal
MSM	Meritorious Service Medal
MVO	Member of the Royal Victorian Order
OBE	Officer of The Most Excellent Order of the British Empire
PSC	Passed Staff College
TD	Territorial Decoration
VC	Victoria Cross

Military Ranks and Appointments

Brig.-Gen.	Brigadier-General
BSM	Band Sergeant Major
Capt.	Captain
Cpl	Corporal
C/Sgt	Colour Sergeant
CSM	Company Sergeant Major
CQMS	Company Quartermaster Sergeant
Pte	Private
L/Cpl	Lance Corporal
Lt	Lieutenant
Lt-Col	Lieutenant-Colonel
Lt-Gen.	Lieutenant-General
Maj.	Major
Maj.-Gen.	Major-General
RSM	Regimental Sergeant Major
RQMS	Regimental Quartermaster Sergeant
Sgt	Sergeant
WOI	Warrant Officer Class I
WOII	Warrant Officer Class II
2/Lt	Second Lieutenant

Bibliography

Published Books

Barton, E.C. *Let the Boy Win His Spurs*, (The Research Publishing Company [Fudge & Co Ltd], 1976)

Birdwood, Lt-Col Lord *The Worcestershire Regiment*, (Gale and Polden Ltd, 1952)

Cannon, R. *Historical record of the Thirty Sixth or Herefordshire Regiment of Foot*, (Parker, Furnivall and Parker, 1853)

Douet, J. *British Barracks 1600-1914*, (Stationery Office, 1998)

Everard, Major H. *History of The 29th (Worcestershire Regiment) Foot*, (Littlebury & Company, 1891)

Everard, Colonel H. *Officers Services 29th Foot 1694-1909*, 3 volumes, Bound Draft Books held in the Regimental Museum Archive

Holden, Captain R. *Historical Record of the 3rd and 4th Battalions of the Worcestershire Regiment*, (Kegan Paul, Trench & Co, 1887)

Mallinson, A. *The History of the British Army*, (Bantam Press, 2009)

May, T. *Military Barracks*, (Shire Publications, 2002)

Priestley, R.E. *Work of the R.E. in the European War, 1914-1918 The Signal Service (France)*, (The Naval & Military Press Ltd, 2006)

Ricketts, Lt-Col J.D. and Patrickson, Lt-Col D.J. *36th Regiment of Foot Record of Officers' Services and Historical Notes 1701-1881*, 2 volumes, produced in-house for the Regimental Museum Archive, (1990)

Selwyn, F. *Hitler's Englishman*, (Penguin Books, 1993)

Smyth, Brigadier J.D. *Milestones,* (Sidgwick & Jackson, 1979)

Stacke, Captain H.FitzM. *Notes on Regimental History*, (W.H. Smith & Son, 1917)
The Worcestershire Regiment in the Great War, (G.T. Cheshire & Sons, 1928)

Taylor, B. *Seide Maises … Grandfathers Tales, (*Normita Press, 1994)

Articles in *The Green 'Un*, The Worcestershire Regimental Magazine

'With The Depot', ed. by Capt. H. FitzM. Stacke, Volume 1, November 1922

'Worcestershire Regimental Annual Reunion', Volume 4, August 1926

Articles in *Firm*, The Worcestershire Regimental Magazine

'The Impressions of a New Recruit', Volume 1, July 1929

'Major H.FitzM. Stacke, MC, PSC', Volume 7, January 1936

Depot Notes, 'The Depot "At Home"', Volume 8, October 1936

Depot Notes, Volume 10, October 1938

Depot Notes, Volume 11, July 1939

Auxiliary Territorial Service Notes, Volume 11, October 1939

'Someone at the Door', Volume 12, April 1940

'The First Militia', Volume 12, April 1940

'Snorting Barracks at War', Volume 12, December 1940

'We Make em Proud', Volume 12, November 1945

'The 1ˢᵗ Battalion Colours, October 24th, 1914', Volume 13, October 1946

Depot Party Notes, Volume 13, January 1947

'Laying up of the Colours of the 2ⁿᵈ Battalion, The Worcestershire Regiment', Volume 14, October 1947

2nd Battalion Notes, Volume 14, October 1947

29 PTC Notes, Football, Volume 15, July 1948

'On the Air', Volume 15, January 1949

'The Home Guard', Volume 15, January 1949

'The Presentation of The Freedom of Entry April 15ᵗʰ 1950', Volume 17, April 1950 (Attached Special and Silver Drums Programme)

'Our Custodian, Mr Frank Lester', Volume 17, July 1950

Obituary, Sergeant Frank Lester (1892-1950), Volume 17, July 1950

Editorial, Volume 17, January 1951

'Anglo-American Occasions', Volume 18, April 1951

'Coronation Activities', Volume 20, April 1953

'Stars of Radio and Television', Volume 20, July 1953

Band Notes, 'Coronation Week', Volume 20, July 1953

'The Last Passing Out Parade at Norton', Volume 26, October 1959

Obituary, CQMS J. Sopp, Volume 29, April 1962

Obituary, Mr (ex-RQMS) F.S. Oldham, Volume 34, January 1967

Obituary, Mr J.T. Parkes, Volume 35, October 1968

Article in *The Outpost*, B Company 1 Battalion Worcestershire Regiment (British Honduras) Magazine
'The Depot – In Retrospect', November 1958

Articles in *Firm and Forester*, The Worcestershire & Sherwood Foresters Regimental Magazine
Obituary, Lieutenant Colonel R.H.M. Lee, Volume 3 (4), October 1975

'14ᵗʰ Signal Regiment' by Capt. R. Holmes, Volume 4 (2), October 1976

Obituary, Major J.M. Graham, Volume 4 (2), October 1976

Obituary, RQMS W.S. Shaw, Volume 7 (2), October 1982

'Esprit de Corps' by A.W. Phasey, Volume 9 (4), October 1987

Letter to the Editor from Mrs E.M. Dalloway, Volume 9 (1), April 1986

'An Indefatigable Worker' by Lt-Col C.P. Love, Volume 10 (3), April 1989

Obituary, Major A. Maycock, Volume 13 (4), November 1995

Regimental News, Norton Barracks, Volume 13 (4), November 1995

Letter from Philip Turner, Volume 13 (4,) November 1995

'Back To My Roots' by J. Bastable, Volume 14 (4), November 1997

Article by Mrs G. Jones, Volume 15 November 1998

'Norton Barracks – Fifty Years On' by Mrs D. Ricketts, Volume 19 (2), November 2006

Personal Accounts, Letters and Notes

Barley, Private W. *My Experience in the Army*, (Extract from his Diary, Original held by the Liddle Collection at the University of Leeds, Ref GS0088. Copy in Regimental Archives)

Beard, S. *Served with Honour, Norton Barracks* Personal Account (Regimental Archives)

Carter, Mr. N.E. *A Brief Account of Recollections At Norton Barracks 1943*, Letter to RHQ dated 12 August 1997 (Regimental Archives)

Deakin, A. Letter to Colonel Lowles dated 13 September 1997 (Regimental Archives)

Dunn, Captain. P. *Some Memories of Norton Barracks*, Handwritten Notes: Autumn 2006 (Regimental Archives)

Dyer, G. *Enlistment,* Typewritten Notes (Regimental Archives)

Dyer, G. *The Years 1939-45,* Typewritten Notes (Regimental Archives)

Galley, Thomas Edward *Boer War Memories of Pte Thomas Edward Galley, MM*, Notes (Regimental Archive)

Galley, Thomas Edward *Think Well Over These, Memories of the Great War 1914-1918*, Notes (Regimental Archive)

Maycock, Major A. *Individual War Diary* (Regimental Archives)

Price, Mrs E.M.J. Notes to Author, 29 May 2013

Priestley, R.E. Service Memories round and about the First World War (Miscellaneous Papers, ref US38/1/2, Special Collections, Cadbury Research Library, University of Birmingham, 1958)

Reynolds, Lieutenant Colonel J.D. *Memories of Norton Barracks 1935-1959,* Typewritten Notes (Regimental Archives)

Sellars, J. *Join the Army and see the World*, undated letter (Regimental Archives)

Spackman, Rev. F. Letter to Editor *Firm*, 10 June 1947

Wilks, M. References to Norton Barracks Found During Home Guard Research (Regimental Archives)

Magazines and Newspapers

Allen, K. 'Raw Recruits at Norton Barracks in 1945' by K. Allen in *The Black Country Bugle*, 9 June 2011

'Concert at Norton Barracks' in *The Evesham Standard*, 20 July 1940

'Where are the Merry Band?' by T. Guest in the *Worcester Standard*, 29 January 2004

'The Village, the Church and the Pub' by R. Millar in *Worcestershire Now*, October 2005

'Memory Lane, Worcester's War Wireless Wonders' by M. Grundy in the *Worcester Evening News*, 10 May 1997

'Memory Lane, Austrian Prisoners who were held near Norton Barracks' by M. Grundy in the *Worcester Evening News*, 7 November 1998

World Wide Web

http//www.worcestershireregiment.com

http//www.hargreave-mawson.demon.co.uk/Portraits.html, accessed 10/11/2012

http//www.norton-juxta-kempsey.co.uk/#/history

Miscellaneous

Jobson, S. '"Best Kit Wins", How Important were Changes in Weapons and Equipment to Eventual British Military Success on the Western Front', MA Essay 4, University of Birmingham (2007)

2nd Battalion Digest of Service

Army Book 358, Particulars of Attestation for 524132 Joyce, William

REFERENCES

The Worcestershire Regiment down the years
1. Some regiments, including Guards regiments, were numbered from 1 to 4
2. S. Jobson '"Best Kit Wins", How Important were Changes in Weapons and Equipment to Eventual British Military Success on the Western Front?', MA Essay 4, University of Birmingham, (January 2007), p.4

1 Building and Occupation, 1874-98
1. Lt-Col Lord Birdwood, *The Worcestershire Regiment*, (Gale & Polden Ltd, 1952), p.244
2. J. Douet, *British Barracks 1600-1914*, (Stationary Office, 1998), p.169
3. Captain R. Holden, *Historical Record of the 3rd and 4th Battalions of the Worcestershire Regiment* (Kegan Paul, Trench & Co, 1887), pp.232-233
4. T. May, *Military Barracks*, (Shire Publications, 2002), p.19
5. *ibid*, p.20
6. Major H. Everard, *History of The 29th (Worcestershire Regiment) Foot* (Littlebury & Company, 1891), p.520
7. *ibid*, p.519
8. *ibid*, p.520
9. Holden, *Historical Record, op.cit.* pp.232-233
10. Lt-Col J.D. Ricketts and Lt-Col D.J. Patrickson, *36th Regiment of Foot Record of Officers' Services and Historical Notes 1701-1881*, (Produced in-house for the Regimental Museum Archive, 1990), pp.154-155
11. R. Cannon, *Historical Record of The Thirty-Sixth or the Herefordshire Regiment of Foot* (Parker, Furnivall, and Parker, 1853), p.26
12. Ricketts, *36th Regiment of Foot Record of Officers' Services, op.cit.* p.155

13. Further training of Regular soldiers was carried out by the battalions
14. Holden, *Historical Record, op.cit.* p.233
15. *ibid*, pp.246, 249, 258

2 The Boer War to the start of the First World War, 1899-1914
1. Captain H.FitzM. Stacke, *Notes on Regimental History*, (W.H. Smith & Son, 1917), p.34
2. Thomas Edward Galley, *Boer War Memories of Pte. Thomas Edward Galley, MM,* notes in the Regimental Archives
3. Captain H.FitzM. Stacke. *The Worcestershire Regiment in the Great War*, (G.T. Cheshire & Sons, 1928) pp.xxxiii-xxix

3 The First World War, 1914-18
1. Stacke, *The Worcestershire Regiment in the Great War, op.cit.* p.1
2. H. Webb, 'The 1st Battalion Colours, October 24th, 1914', *Firm* ,Volume 13, October 1946, p.251
3. A common term of engagement saw men enlisted for 12 years, 7 with the colours followed by 5 on reserve
4. Thomas Edward Galley, *Think Well over these Memories of the Great War 1914-1918*, notes in the Regimental Archives
5. Stacke, *The Worcestershire Regiment in the Great War, op.cit.* pp.1-2, 42
6. *ibid*, p.45
7. Private W. Barley, *My Experience in the Army*, extract from his Diary a copy of which is held in the Regimental Archives
8. R.E. Priestley, *Work of the R.E. in the European War, 1914-1918 The Signal Service (France),* (The Naval & Military Press Ltd, 2006), p.168

9. R. Priestley, *Service Memories round and about the First World War*, (Miscellaneous papers, Ref US38/1/2 Special Collections Cadbury Research Library University of Birmingham 1958), pp.6-8

10. *ibid*

11. M. Grundy, 'Memory Lane, Worcester's War Wireless Wonders', *Worcester Evening News*, 10 May 1997, p.18

12. Stacke, *The Worcestershire Regiment in the Great War*, *op.cit.* p.44

13. *ibid*, p.46

14. M. Grundy, 'Memory Lane, Austrian Prisoners Who Were Held Near Norton Barracks', *Worcester Evening News*, 7 November 1998, p.21

4 The Depot between the wars, 1919-39

1. Lt R. Newcomb, Major J.M. Graham Obituary, *Firm and Forester*, Volume 4 (2), October 1976, p.23

2. F. Selwyn, *Hitler's Englishman*, (Penguin Books, 1993), p.22

3. Army Book 358 Particulars of Attestation 5245132 William Joyce

4. J. Sellars, *Join the Army and see the World*, undated letter (Regimental Archives)

5. A.W. Phasey, 'Esprit de Corps', *Firm and Forester*, Volume 9 (4), October 1987, pp.316-317

6. 'The Impressions of a New Recruit', *Firm*, Volume 1, July 1929, p.352

7. G. Dyer, *Enlistment*, from notes held in the Regimental Archives

8. A. Deakin, *Letter to Colonel Lowles* dated 13 September 1997 (Regimental Archives)

9. Depot Notes 'The Depot "At Home"', *Firm*, Volume 8, October 1936, pp.397-401

10. E.C. Barton, *Let the Boy Win His Spurs* (The Research Publishing Company [Fudge & Co Ltd], 1976), p.125

11. Field Marshal Sir C.W. Jacob, GCB, KCSI, KCMG, 'Major H.FitzM. Stacke, MC', *Firm*, Volume 7, January 1936, pp.401-403

12. *ibid*; Lt-Col C.P. Love, TD, 'An Indefatigable Worker', *Firm and Forester*, Volume 10 (3), pp.246-48

13. Birdwood, *The Worcestershire Regiment*, *op.cit.* pp.253, 254

14. Depot Notes, *Firm*, Volume 10, October 1938, p.455

15. F.W. Mulley, 'The First Militia', *Firm*, Volume 12, April 1940, p.25

16. Depot Notes, *Firm*, Volume 11, July 1939, p.285

17. *ibid*

18. *ibid*, p.287

19. *ibid*, pp.291-292

20. Auxiliary Territorial Service Notes, *Firm*, Volume 11, October 1939, pp.398-401

5 The Second World War, 1939-45

1. Birdwood, *The Worcestershire Regiment*, p.244

2. *ibid*, p.244

3. G. Dyer, *The Years 1939-45*, notes (Regimental Archives)

4. S. Beard, *Served with Honour, Norton Barracks*, Personal Account, (Regimental Archives)

5. Major A Maycock, *Individual War Diary*, (Regimental Archives)

6. M. Wilks, References to Norton Barracks Found During Home Guard Research, (Regimental Archives)

7. Major A. Shelley Creak, 'The Home Guard', *Firm*, Volume 15, January 1949, p.316

8. 'Snorting Barracks at War', *Firm*, Volume 12 December 1940, p.92

9. Mrs E.M.J. Price (Daughter of Sgt Curly Dalloway), notes to Author, 29 May 2013

10. Obituary, Lt-Colonel R.H. Melville-Lee, OBE, *Firm and Forester*, Volume 3 (4), October 1975, p.18

11. Brigadier J.D. Smyth, VC, *Milestones*, (Sidgwick & Jackson, 1979), p.142

12. S. Beard, *Served with Honour, Norton Barracks*, personal account, (Regimental Archives)

13. K. Allen, 'Raw Recruits at Norton Barracks in 1945', *Black Country Bugle*, 9 Jun 2011

14. 'Concert at Norton Barracks', *The Evesham Standard*, 20 July 1940

15. As officers names could not be published during the war he went under the stage name of John Darwin

16. 'Someone at the Door', *Firm*, Volume 12, April 1940, pp.67-68

17. Colonel J.D. Reynolds, *Memories of Norton Barracks 1935-1959*, typed notes (Regimental Archive)
18. http//www.worcestershireregiment.com
19. Obituary, Lt-Colonel R.H. Melville-Lee, OBE, *Firm and Forester*, Volume 4 (4), October 1975
20. *ibid*
21. Reynolds, *Memories of Norton Barracks 1935-1959, op.cit.*
22. Major H.P.E. Pereira, *The Home of the Worcestershire Regiment*, Extract (Regimental Archives)
23. Brigadier B.C.S. Clarke, 'We Make em Proud', *Firm*, Volume 12, November 1945, pp.332-336
24. Mr N.E. Carter, *A Brief Account of Recollections at Norton Barracks 1943*, Letter to RHQ 12 August 1997 (Regimental Archive)
25. Mrs E.M.J. Price, notes
26. Obituary, Major A. Maycock, *Firm and Forester*, Volume 13 (4), November 1995, p.386
27. Major A. Maycock, *Individual War Diary*, (Regimental Archives)
28. B. Taylor, *Seide Maise s... Grandfathers Tales*, (Normita Press, 1994), p.180
29. K. Allen, 'Raw Recruits at Norton Barracks in 1945', *The Black Country Bugle*, 9 June 2011

6 The Final Years

1. Birdwood, *The Worcestershire Regiment, op.cit.* p.245
2. Revd F. Spackman, Letter to the editor of *Firm* 10 June 1947
3. 2nd Battalion Notes, *Firm*, Volume 14, October 1947, p.212
4. 'Laying up of the Colours of the 2nd Battalion, The Worcestershire Regiment', *Firm*, Volume 14, October 1947, p.231
5. Birdwood, *The Worcestershire Regiment, op.cit.* p.246
6. *ibid*
7. 'The Presentation of the "Freedom of Entry and Silver Drums April 15th 1950', *Firm*, Volume 17, April 1950, (Attached Special Programme), pp.5-27
8. Editorial, *Firm*, Volume 17, January 1951, p.143
9. 'Anglo-American Occasions', *Firm*, Volume 18 April 1951, p.7
10. Mrs E.M.J. Price, notes
11. Obituary, RQMS W.S. Shaw, *Firm and Forester*, Volume 7 (2), October 1982, p.149
12. Obituary, CQMS J. Sopp, *Firm*, Volume 29 April 1962, p.16
13. Captain. P. Dunn, *Some Memories of Norton Barracks*, handwritten notes: Autumn 2006, p.21a, (Regimental Archives)
14. Sgt, later WOII, F. 'Juggy' Jones
15. Philip Turner Letter, *Firm and Forester*, Volume 13 (4), November 1995, p.306
16. Reynolds, *Memories of Norton Barracks 1935-1959, op.cit.*
17. 'On the Air', *Firm*, Volume 15, January 1949, pp.280-281
18. 'Stars of Radio and Television', *Firm*, Volume 20, July 1953, pp102-105
19. Reginald William Winchester Wilmot, an Australian war correspondent for the BBC and the Australian Broadcasting Corporation during the Second World War. Afterwards he continued to work as a broadcast reporter. He was killed when a BOAC Comet airliner crashed over the Mediterranean on 10 January 1954
20. 'Coronation Activities', *Firm*, Volume 20, April 1953, p.15
21. Band Notes, 'Coronation Week', *Firm*, Volume 20, July 1953, pp.112-114
22. Mrs D. Ricketts, 'Norton Barracks – Fifty Years On', *Firm and Forester*, Volume 19 (2), November 2006, p.121
23. When two men have the same rank and name it is customary to identify them by the last two digits of their regimental number
24. Mrs D. Ricketts, 'Norton Barracks – Fifty Years On', *op.cit.* p.121
25. The other being C/Sgt J. Sopp
26. 'The last Passing Out Parade at Norton?', *Firm*, Volume 26, October 1959, p.147
27. Mr A. Mackie, note to Col Lowles

7 The Depot – In Retrospect

1. 'The Depot – In Retrospect', *The Outpost*, ('B' Company 1Bn Worcestershire Regiment, British Honduras, Regimental Magazine) November 1958

8 Sport and Other Activities

1. 29 PTC Notes Football, *Firm*, Volume 15 July 1948, p.180
2. Mrs E M. Dalloway, Letter to the Editor, *Firm and Forester*, Volume 9 (1), April 1986, p.20
3. T. Guest, 'Where are the Merry Band', *The Worcester Standard*, 29 January 2004, p.12
4. Obituary Major J.M. Graham by Lt-Col E.R. Newcomb, *Firm and Forester*, Volume 4 (2), October 1976, p.23
5. Regimental anecdote via John Lowles
6. Mrs D. Ricketts, 'Norton Barracks – Fifty Years On', *Firm and Forester*, Volume 19, November 2006, p.121
7. Mrs E.M.J. Price, manuscript notes

9 Regimental Headquarters

1. Captain R. Holmes, '14th Signal Regiment', *Firm and Forester*, Volume 4 (2), October 1976, p.33
2. *ibid*, pp.33-35
3. Regimental News, 'Norton Barracks', *Firm and Forester*, Volume 13 (4), November 1995, pp.294-295
4. Mrs G. Jones, *Firm and Forester*, Volume 15, November 1998, p.97

10 The Depot and Norton Parish Church

1. http://www.norton-juxta-kempsey.co.uk/#/history

11 The Regimental Museum

1. Capt. H.FitzM. Stacke (ed.), 'With the Depot', *The Green 'Un*, Volume 1, November 1922, p.17
2. Birdwood, *The Worcestershire Regiment, op.cit.* p.254
3. *ibid*
4. Obituary, Sergeant Frank Lester (1892-1950), *Firm*, Volume 17, July 1950, pp.61-62

12 Aftermath – The Barracks site now

1. J. Bastable, 'Back To My Roots', *Firm and Forester*, Volume 14 (4), November 1997, p.277
2. Mrs D. Ricketts, *Norton Barracks – Fifty Years On, op.cit.* p.121
3. J.D. Reynolds, *Memories of Norton Barracks 1935-1959, op.cit.*

Index of Names

(Numbers in italics indicate illustrations)

General Index
(Numbers in italics indicate illustrations)